What Others Are Saying

about Endurance 101

"I wish I had this book when I discovered endurance riding!" – **Julie Suhr,** endurance legend and author of ***Ten Feet Tall, Again***

• • •

"If the sport of Endurance Riding has intrigued, or intimidated you, *Endurance 101* is the next best thing to a two-legged mentor. Aarene unravels the mysteries of getting you and your horse to the starting line, through your first ride, and through what happens afterwards, always with the goals of caring properly for your horse and having fun. The book is geared toward beginners, but it's also a humorous, delightful, and useful read for the established endurance rider who knows everything but might have forgotten something along the way." – **Merri Melde,** equestrian photographer and endurance journalist, writer at ***The Equestrian Vagabond***

• • •

"Giddy up! *Endurance 101* is stuffed full of details to help riders to get their feet wet distance riding. Read this book, then cinch 'er up tight and git 'er done!" – **Dennis Summers,** author of ***4th Gear – Power up Your Endurance Horse***

• • •

"For all you newbies or wannabes, this is the book for you. Aarene covers all the basics including tips from the "Bad Idea Fairy" – **Sue Summers**, co-author of ***4th Gear – Power up Your Endurance Horse***

• • •

"The hardest thing about joining a new sport is knowing how to get started. Aarene Storms allows what seems impossible to become a possibility. Anyone interested in joining the rigorous sport of endurance riding receives a friendly & encouraging look into making it happen by reading *Endurance 101*." – **Robert "Trailmeister" Eversole,** equestrian writer at ***www.trailmeister.com***

• • •

"Informative? Check.

Useful? Check.

Did I learn stuff about horses I didn't know before? Check.

Did it make me laugh? Check.

Oh, yeah, and it also taught me about endurance riding.

This is a simple, straightforward, extremely easy read (the author has a great writing style that makes learning FUN), and I heartily recommend it. If you've ever been curious about endurance, want to learn a few tips about horse care and conditioning, or want a nice read about horses chock full of some laughs, I heartily recommend this book." – **Becky Bean,** novice endurance rider

ENDURANCE 101

a gentle guide to the sport of long-distance riding

by Aarene Storms

photos by Monica Bretherton

TRIANGLE RANCH COMMUNICATIONS

ENDURANCE 101: a gentle guide to the sport of long-distance riding

is a publication of Triangle Ranch Communications

Editor: Anne Doe Overstreet

ISBN 978-0-9885519-1-6

THIS BOOK WAS PRINTED IN THE U.S.A.

Triangle Ranch Communications is a micropress based in Seattle, WA.

publisher@triangleranch.com

www.endurance-101.com

Acknowledgements

It's taken more than ten years for author Aarene Storms to learn enough to write this book, and more than a year to write it, and more than a few hundred people helped her do it. These are the names she can remember.

First off: A million gazillion bazillion thanks to the family members who never stopped encouraging: "Santa Jim," Will and Lisa Beidle, Barbara, North, and Randall Storms.

And also:

Anne Doe Overstreet, Becky Bean, Bev Borton, Cathy Leddy, Charles deLint, Connie Hoge, Darlene Anderson, David LeBlanc, Deborah Schneider, Dennis Summers, Diana Ball, Dick Borton, Dory Jackson, Duana Kolouskova, Elizabeth Funderburk, Ellen Harvey, Gail Williams, Greener Pastures Adoption Agency, Jacqui Gallant, Jennifer LeBlanc, Jennifer Strelkauskas DVM, Jillian Zemanek, Julie Suhr, Katie Milholland, Laura Crum, Lori Hudson, Madeline Smart, Meagan Hudson, Merri Melde, Mike Williams, Patty Robinett DVM, Paul Latiolais, Ron Hayden, Ron Silvern, Ryan Williams, Sirie Neal Michaels, Sky Evans, Sue Brown, Susan Garlinghouse DVM, Susan Summers, Susan Thornberg, Tiffany Sampson LaPlante, Trish Chomyn and Troy Smith.

And let's not forget the horses...

Endurance 101 is dedicated by Aarene:

"To all the horses who have carried me so far: Story, Bo, the Toad, Laser, Blaze, Hana and especially Fiddle."

Photographer Monica Bretherton wishes to thank her own family as well as everybody who participated in the photography sessions -- most particularly, the cover models, Abby and Emma Byers, Sky Evans and Katie Milholland and their trusty steeds, and Danny, Hana and Kheema for being reliable "tripod horses."

Table of Contents

The first ride of the Northwest Region, Home on the Range, seen through the ears of Magdan (Danny).

INTRODUCTION

One horse. One rider. One very long trail.

This is the essence of the sport of endurance riding: spending a long time on a long trail with a horse.

Some people ride with friends, others ride solo. The trails traverse rolling hills, mountains, deserts, or even city streets. As long as a trail is safe for horses, it might be used for an endurance ride. Some of the most beautiful wilderness areas in America can be enjoyed from the back of your horse during an endurance event.

There are veterinary checkpoints along the route, where horses are evaluated and given a chance to eat, drink, and rest before heading back out, refreshed and ready, onto the trail.

If this sounds like fun, keep reading!

There is no required or restricted tack in the sport of endurance. There is no required or prohibited gear for riders, either. The riders need only suit themselves, their mount, the terrain, and their own budgets.

This book will make some suggestions about choosing horses and gear, but the most important part of the equation is you, the rider. Do you want to spend hours each week in training, and hours on competition day with your friends and your horse out on trails that may leave you hungry, thirsty, tired, cranky, sunburned (or cold)...and almost invariably, grinning from ear-to-ear?

If the answer is "yes," then you are a future endurance rider!

Endurance is unlike many other equestrian competitions because it is possible for every competitor to "win" the ride. The American Endurance Ride Conference (AERC) has a very unusual motto: "To Finish is to Win."

In other words: all horse-and-rider teams to finish the course in the time allowed with approval by the attending veterinarian(s) are awarded a prize and mileage points, including the team that finishes dead last.

Some rides even give a special award to the "turtle" or last-place finisher.

Riders are not subject to age, health or ability restrictions. Some riders are as young as 5 or 6 years old. Junior riders (age 16 or younger) must ride with a "sponsor"—a responsible adult over the age of 21. Some riders are in their 70's—or even 80's. Riders can be cancer survivors, diabetics, or heart transplant recipients. At least one current competitor is a double amputee. Endurance riders have this in common: they are people who enjoy a challenge that is both mental and physical. Even more, endurance riders are people who are dedicated to spending the time needed to create a deep bond with a horse on some of the most beautiful trails on the planet.

The endurance community is known for a friendly, helpful attitude toward both experienced competitors and brand-new riders. It's often easy for beginners to find people who will help select a first event, and get ready to compete—and now, there is a book to help as well.

This book is written for riders new to the sport of endurance. It gives guidance about choosing an endurance mount (he might be in your pasture already), choosing tack, beginning your training, and competing safely. There is a special section for junior riders, and lots of photos to illustrate concepts. And, just for fun, there are a few sections describing the endurance career of the "Bad Idea Fairy", who always manages to make the wrong choices.

If endurance sounds like fun to you, then settle back and prepare to enjoy this gentle introduction to the extreme sport of long-distance riding!

RIDE
CAMP

Four successful endurance equines (clockwise from top left): Junior (with Max Merlich), mule – 3560 AERC miles, 2009 Tevis completion. Lucero Reedo De Rioto (with Paul Latiolais), Paso Fino – 2315 AERC miles. The Fury (with Garrett Ford), Arabian – 980 AERC miles, multiple Tevis top-ten completions, including 2012 winner and Best Condition award. Patrickhan (with Jas Shearer-McMahon), Akhal-Teke – 1545 AERC miles, 2011 Tevis completion.

CHAPTER 1

FIND THE RIGHT HORSE

Finding the right horse for a begining endurance rider is easier than you think. Do you already have a horse? Is he sound? Can he carry a rider? And is he willing and able to move down the trail with you? If so, you may have already found your beginning endurance horse! There are few hard and fast rules about what sort of equines can participate in the sport of endurance riding.

In this chapter, we cover the basics of selecting an appropriate horse. We will take a look at conformation, a frequent worry for some riders, and examine photos of horses that are competing successfully in the sport. We will also discuss which factors are non-negotiable in selecting an endurance horse, that is, which horses are suited to the sport, and which horses should be allowed to do another sport instead.

AERC Rules and Requirements

The American Endurance Ride Conference (AERC) rulebook has little to say about the rules and requirements for selecting an endurance horse. Ponies, draft horses, gaited horses, mules, even zebras are eligible to participate. You could ride a unicorn, if you could find one willing to carry you all day long.

1.1: AERC Rules

- The ride must be open to any breed or type of equine.
- The equines entered in the full distances must be at least 60 months old at the time of the ride.
- Equines must be at least 48 months old at the time of the ride [for Limited Distance events of less than 50 miles].
- Age is figured from actual date of birth, not the universal "racehorse birthday" of January 1st in a given year, as is the case for Thoroughbred racers. In the absence of papers, a ride veterinarian's opinion and discretion must prevail.

A horse must be at least 5 years old to participate in endurance events of 50 miles or longer, and must be at least 4 years old to participate in limited distance events. Endurance is not a sport that "washes out" horses after they turn 5 (or 7 or 20) years old. In many cases an older, more experienced horse is a savvier competitor than a younger horse.

Although some equines are better suited to the sport than others, all are welcome at the start line, as long as they meet a few basic requirements, such as the "age at time of the event" requirement. Distance is also a factor. "The full distance" is a ride of 50 miles or longer. "Limited distance" (or LD) events are 25 miles or longer, but shorter than 50 miles. Most LD events are 25 to 30 miles long.

Endurance is not a sport for baby horses.

The concussion of miles of trails and the demands the sport makes on a horse's metabolism should only be asked of full-grown horses. Because of concern over this, there is an ongoing discussion within the organization about increasing the minimum age for participation to age 6 for endurance and age 5 for limited distance.

Endurance horses, unlike flat-track racers, are often in their prime around age 12 to 15; some horses compete for 10 years or more. The famous competitor Elmer Bandit competed well into his mid-thirties, although he is considered extraordinary.

After competing in endurance for more than ten years and four thousand miles, B.R. Cody de Soi placed second at the arduous 100-mile Tevis ride in 2011.

Conformation preferences and requirements

"But," you ask yourself, "don't I need an Arabian horse to do endurance?"

The short answer is "NO." Many breeds compete successfully in endurance each year.

The long answer begins with a grammar lesson.

***Conformation.* Say it with me: "Con-*FOR*-may-shun."**

The definition of confirmation is the establishing [of something] as true; ratification; verification. Conformation, on the other hand, is the structure or *form* of a thing.

I hereby conFIRM that the conFORmation of your horse is something to consider when you consider the sport of endurance.

Now that we've defined the terms and gotten that pesky business out of the way (and now that everybody reading this will use the two words correctly in print forever after, and forever avoid the wrath of the ghost of my university grammar professor) we can move on to an examination of a properly conformed endurance horse.

The Ideal Endurance Horse

The ideal animal stands between 13 and 18 hands tall and can be either dainty of form or sturdy of form or average in form; in gender the equine should be male, female or some neutered form of either.

The horse shall preferably have more than three feet, but less than five, and should have a tail located at the end of the body furthest from the nose.

Although purple is ideal, other permitted colors include black, brown, red, grey, painted, pocked, spotted, mottled, speckled or bluish green. Mixing of the permitted colors is allowed; other colors are allowed on a hardship basis.

All silliness aside, there is much truth (which I can *confirm*) in the statements above.

When it comes to the size and build of a beginner's endurance horse, I urge the reader to simply look out in the pasture to see what is standing there. If there's a horse that is willing and able to carry you down the trail, then, by all means, start with him.

Is your horse a suitable endurance prospect?

Julie Suhr, the acclaimed Grande Dame of Endurance, says that her ideal endurance horse is "short, sane, and smooth" (Suhr, 2002). Although not everyone places the same value on these traits, they are qualities to keep in mind.

Short. Your endurance horse should be big enough to carry you, but a long, large, or tall rider does not necessarily need a gigantic horse. If the rider feels that there is enough horse between the saddle and the ground, and if the horse is comfortable carrying the weight of the rider and tack, the horse is big enough. Larger riders may wish to seek a larger-boned steed, rather than a taller one.

If you are not tall, consider choosing a horse under 15 hands. Your horse will not get shorter at Milepost 20 so that you can hop on easily (I have tested this extensively, and found that, in fact, my horse seems to get taller after 40 miles). Vertically challenged riders would be wise to choose either a small horse or one that allows rocks, stumps, and the fenders of random trucks to be used as mounting blocks.

Smooth. Although the vast majority of horses currently competing in endurance are Arabians or Arab crosses, as the average age of endurance riders climbs, so does the popularity of easy-gaited horse breeds, such as Missouri Fox Trotters, Paso Finos, and Tennessee Walking Horses (AERC registration records, 2012). Even diminutive Icelandic horses are showing up in the sport, their riders gliding down the trails at a rapid ambling tolt.

If you prefer a two-beat trot, seek out a horse whose footfalls are quiet, rather than one who pounds the ground. Look for a gliding, springy motion when you watch the horse move. In general, you will be most comfortable over time and distance with one who rides more like a Cadillac than a jackhammer.

Sane. This is a matter of personal preference. I have ridden a dingbat and I have ridden a horse who exemplifies sensibility, and I prefer Team Sensible. However, if you are offered the choice between a sensible horse who bores you to tears and a dingbat who leaves you grinning after every ride, then take my blessings and saddle up the dingbat. In the process of training and competing with your horse, the two of you will form strong emotional bonds, as well as strong muscles. Choose a horse that you enjoy spending time with in as well as out of the saddle.

Certainly, if you get serious about the sport and decide to start training for world-class events, you may want to obtain a more perfectly conformed specimen.

This Rocky Mountain mare has a smooth easy-gait.

That, however, can wait. For your first season or two, if he's up to the challenge, give Old Reliable a try. You can always buy or borrow another horse later. Who knows? If you enjoy riding Reliable over barrels or around jumps, the two of you may have years of fun on the trails ahead.

Get a vet's opinion

No matter what horse you choose, consult an endurance vet about the suitability of your horse for the sport. Although vets in general are wonderful and useful people, an *endurance* vet is one who has spent more than one weekend—and preferably more than 5 years—in the sport working at endurance rides. An endurance vet will have evaluated hundreds of endurance horses, and will be able to give you good advice about the physical suitability of your horse for the sport.

A veterinary exam should focus on soundness (X-rays are a reasonable expense) and metabolic sturdiness. Your vet will not be able to guarantee that your endurance prospect will be a long-distance superstar, but can point out physical shortcomings that may cause problems on the trail. You will rarely hear that a particular horse is completely unsuitable for the sport; rather, a competent endurance vet will be able to recommend strategies for helping the individual animal thrive during sustained distance work.

Focus on soundness

Strong legs and feet are essential for a long-distance mount, because trotting hundreds of training miles creates a lot of concussion. There is a saying among endurance riders: *"sound enough" isn't sound enough for endurance.* In other words, a horse with old tendon injuries, a wonky knee, a tendency to abscess, or any other recurring lameness issues should look for a different job. However, old/cold splints—no matter how ugly—are not a concern for endurance horses.

Your horse must be consistently well-trimmed or shod. I cannot over-emphasize this. Your endurance prospect should not start training until his feet are in good shape, with strong, healthy horn and a balanced trim. If he wears steel shoes, the shoes need to be applied properly and replaced regularly. There are places that one can cut expenses in endurance, but foot care is not one of them. Determine the best hoof-protection option for your particular horse and don't be afraid to bake cookies every 5 to 8 weeks to send along with the check for the farrier. If your horse travels barefoot or booted, learn to recognize a strong, balanced trim or to fit his boots properly and replace them when they show signs of excessive wear.

Form follows function. A horse with a "greyhound" or "radiator" build will be superior at cooling compared to a horse with a stocky build. This is important as an endurance horse generates an astonishing amount of heat (which must be dissipated) during a competition. However, the shape of a horse's muscles—actually, the shape of the entire body—will change over time to better suit the work, so don't discard your big-boned horse immediately. *Substance* can be a good thing, and a canny rider can assist a large-muscled horse in staying cool. (This will be addressed more specifically in Chapter 11).

Sue Summers' heavy-duty mount AM Humvee is a Curly horse with more than 3,500 AERC miles and a Tevis completion.

In fact, the ideal build of an endurance horse differs depending on the terrain where the horse regularly works. Larger, bulkier muscles are often seen on horses who win the mountainous Tevis ride, while a longer, stringier appearance is more common among horses in flat desert rides. Grey or light-colored horses are considered easier to cool during bright or hot rides; however, dark-skinned horses can do the work as well, if the rider is prepared to actively aid the cooling process.

Choose a survivor or learn to manage a worrier

No matter what the terrain, endurance horses need to take care of themselves during a long day of work. They must be willing to eat and drink whenever food and water is offered, be willing to relax and rest at vet checks even as other horses and people and machines create a chaotic and non-restful environment, and be willing to return to the task and continue down the trail after a rest break. A horse with a fretful temperament can do the work, but will need your careful attention to guard against metabolic problems. If your horse is a worrier, enlist the help of your vet and trainer; these people may be able to suggest a feed, exercise, and training regimen to help a dither-prone equine.

A competent endurance horse has a long attention span and doesn't spend a lot of energy spooking or worrying. This can be taught with patience and practice, but if your back yard horse has already impressed you with an ability to concentrate while surrounded by noise and confusion, then hand the good creature a carrot and move forward with your training.

If you don't already have a horse in the back yard and are faced with a field full of prospects, choose a horse you enjoy riding and spending time with. An endurance ride is not just a long event; it is a strenuous event that requires a horse and rider team to spend a *lot* of time together every week in the time leading up to a competition. Some endurance riders spend significantly more time with a horse than with a spouse. So if you must choose between an adequate mount that makes you smile and an athletic phenom who gives you nightmares, by all means, choose Mr. Adequate and leave the phenom for somebody who likes that kind of challenge.

World-class endurance horse Monk shows beauty, strength, and fitness.

Equine deal breakers

Notice that I do not emphasize measuring the size of a prospect's cannon bones, or resting heart rate, or the angle of the shoulder or croup. There are only two criteria that I consider deal breakers when selecting a horse for beginning endurance riders:

The horse is unsound or has a long history of lameness. Endurance is hard work. If the horse you are considering isn't sturdy enough to cover long miles, you will only cause him pain and yourself heartache. Find a horse with good feet and legs for this sport.

The horse hates trails. Just as there are people who prefer to spend their days indoors, there are horses that truly prefer working in an arena. It would be unkind to force an arena-loving horse to spend days on the trail. There are many trail-loving horses in the world that would enjoy the work.

Okay then. Let's assume there are no red flags.

Now. Ride the horse. Are you comfortable? Happy? Do you and the horse have fun together?

Your endurance prospect is often nearer than you think. And, tall or short, sturdy or slender, sensible or silly, there is room in the endurance universe for horses—and riders—of all kinds.

The Bad Idea Fairy finds a horse

I am the Bad Idea Fairy (giggle!) and my horse is a super-special Purpaloosa, a very rare breed. The breeder tells me that he is extra-special, so he was extra-expensive. Hops is a stallion, because I want to breed lots of Purpaloosas and get very rich.

Purpaloosas are specially bred to look pretty in pictures. Awesome, right?

When I was shopping for a horse, I saw a lot of ordinary horses; you know, brown, black, grey. BORING! So when I saw the ad for a Purpaloosa Stallion, I knew I had to have him. His picture looked exactly like the pictures from my favorite coloring book when I was little. We were destined to be together.

The breeder wanted me to watch Hops move and maybe ride him a little to see if we were suited before I bought him, but I didn't need to do that. His turquoise mane is exactly the right color to go with my new outfit! His feet are kinda funny shaped, but I think I can put sparkly nail polish on and they will look fine.

Purpaloosas are known for their special gaits: the Trollop™ and the Cantelope™. I don't know how to ride them yet, but I will Google it. Then I'll be really good at it and probably win awards and they might even put a picture of me and Hops on Wikipedia.

Hops' registered name is HOLDMYBEERANDWATCHTHIS, but my BFF took one look at him moving and said, He HOPS! Which is such a cute name I decided to keep it. Isn't that sweet?

Four saddles suitable for endurance (clockwise from top left):

Ansur Excel (treeless); Wintec dressage (synthetic); Specialized

International (customizable panels); Australian stock saddle.

CHAPTER 2
FIND THE RIGHT TACK (FOR HORSE AND RIDER)

Finding the right horse for endurance may be easier than you think. Finding the right tack can be just as simple: start by looking in your barn. Is there a saddle there? A bridle? That's a good place to start.

Although the AERC has no rules whatsoever about required or prohibited tack for endurance competitions, it's worth your time to see what the experienced competitors use. A long trail is the worst place to discover that your tack makes your horse (or your knees) too sore to continue. You won't need to mortgage the farm to find good equipment, but you should pay close attention and be willing to try different options to keep you and your equine partner comfortable. This chapter examines endurance tack in detail, and the last part of the chapter is designed to help you choose gear for yourself and your horse that will keep you safe on the trail and in bad weather.

No matter what tack you choose, however, make this your top priority:

IT MUST FIT.

Technically, after that last sentence, I should power off my computer and go for a ride. The rest of this chapter is just details and variations on that single sentence.

There really is no substitute for tack that fits. You can buy space-age materials, ultra-light designs, or color-coordinated everything in the latest styles. Or you can copy the tack selections of your favorite equestrian hero who has won every ride you've ever heard about for the last 20 years. It will still be inferior to tack that *fits.*

There is a problem with tack that fits, however. To paraphrase the Greek philosopher Heraclitus, "you can never ride the same horse twice." Over months or years of training in long-distance trail work, your horse will change shape dramatically. Your horse already changes shape slightly every day, depending on the amount and quality of his feed, the type and duration of his daily training, and the amount of time he spends on pasture. Even the seasonal changes in his hair coat can affect fit.

The good news is that everybody experiences this. So, theoretically, we all could hold a gigantic Mad Tea Party tack trade two or three times a year, and everyone could just swap gear until they found stuff to fit.

Alas, in the real world, tack fitting is a bit more complicated than that.

So what can you do? My advice? Do the best you can with what you've got.

2.1: AERC Rules

AERC rules and regulations do not include requirements or exclusions regarding equipment or tack you use on your horse and yourself. You can use whatever you want... or nothing at all.

But, hey. At least wear some sunscreen, will ya? Thanks.?

Saddle type, saddle fit

Saddle fit is crucial. If you ride your horse in a saddle that pinches his shoulders or rubs his back, he won't fall over dead, but he may travel with his back hollowed or his hips angled strangely, or contort in any one of the million different ways horses contort to avoid showing pain.

If you don't notice the contortions for a long time, your horse may eventually show up lame, which is just a visible symptom of the need for a better-fitting saddle. This will probably be followed by extensive re-training and dressage practice, as well as chiropractic treatments to get his body back into alignment again.

If you have access to a professional saddle fitter with a computer sensor pad, by all means, take advantage of it! For those of us who don't have access to that kind of expertise, there are some workarounds.

Evaluate your saddle fit by running the flat of your hand under it when your horse is standing squarely with the saddle on his back, but not tightly cinched. Your hand should ideally fit uniformly under the saddle without getting "caught" by a tight spot or being "freed" by an empty spot.

Ask a friend to repeat this evaluation when you are sitting in the saddle. Remember, rider weight makes a difference.

If your horse were entered in a "standing still with a saddle and a rider" competition, you would now be finished with your fitting exercises. However, endurance is a sport of *motion*, and you need to evaluate the fit of your saddle on a moving horse.

You could easily pay a lot of money for a "cookie dough" pad. These pads are infinitely re-usable, so if you are trying to fit tack for a bunch of horses, or if you have a bunch of friends who want to fit tack, it might be a good investment. Place the cookie dough pad between your saddle and the horse and go for a ride. When you're done, carefully remove the saddle and examine the pad. The flexible clay filling inside the pad will be squeezed thin where your saddle is tight and will be thick where your saddle bridges. If there are no dramatic thin or thick spots, you will know that your saddle fits adequately. Keep in mind that the cookie dough pad gives you immediate insight into the fit of *that saddle* with *that rider* over *that terrain.*

A cheaper version of the cookie dough pad can be made with ordinary office supply bubble wrap. Get some spray adhesive and stick a sheet of bubble wrap (big bubbles work best) to a thin saddle pad. Saddle up and go for a ride. When you return, examine the bubble wrap: burst or stretched-thin bubbles (you can feel the texture with your fingers after removing the saddle) indicate where your saddle is too tight.

Don't give up. Getting it right matters. Borrow saddles from friends, use the free trials available at tack stores and experiment with saddle pads. An older saddle with leather that has already been broken in may offer a smart, low-cost choice.

Yes, it can be frustrating, sometimes, but everyone else has to do it too. Sorry. People who tell you differently are probably selling something—most likely, they're selling a saddle.

There is good news: The first year of competition you need not feel obligated to drop Big Bucks on a saddle since your horse will change shape as he grows into the sport. It may take two or three *years* for a horse's body to grow into "fit" shape, so don't blow your saddle budget in the first six months.

Some riders prefer a narrow twist; others prefer a wider, flatter seat. Some riders won't leave home without a saddle horn; others want English-style stirrup leathers that swing freely.

I purposely don't recommend a particular brand or style of saddle. English, Western, Aussie, treed or treeless—any variation of any of these is perfectly permissible for the sport of endurance, as long as the horse and rider are comfortable.

And remember, you're going to be spending a lot of time with that saddle next to a very (*cough*) important location on your own body. When you've found a saddle that fits your horse, make sure it's comfortable for the rider, too! A fleece or foam "seat saver" may be helpful, but if the saddle doesn't fit you very well, your equitation will suffer—and so will you.

Test ride in as many saddles as you can, and choose the style that suits you best. If you already own something that has worked well for you in the past, try that first.

Stirrups

Many endurance and trail riders advocate the use of wide-tread "endurance-style" stirrups, which offer a much larger surface for the rider's foot. The larger foot bed can help prevent foot numbness and nerve pain, so if you suffer from foot discomfort, changing your stirrups may offer significant relief.

Stirrup cages are considered by some to be an essential piece of safety equipment. If you prefer to ride in sneakers or hiking boots without a cut-out heel, or if you habitually ride with your toes pointed down, stirrup cages will prevent your foot from sliding all the way through the stirrup—a hazard if you should fall from your horse. Cages also protect your feet from spiny branches if you ride in thick country.

Many riders prefer the security of stirrup safety cages.

Saddle pad

If your saddle fits, your saddle pad does not need to be anything special, as long as it fits properly under the saddle, is relatively easy to clean, and is tolerated by your horse. A treeless saddle may require a special pad—check with the saddle manufacturer for recommendations.

A horse with thin or sensitive skin may need a natural wool saddle pad. If you use wool, spend the extra money to buy a good quality wool pad if possible; a thickly-woven pad without burrs or lumps in it will last for many miles.

There are plenty of synthetic materials available, as well. If you choose one of these, be sure that the pad does not create or hold heat in against the horse's skin. Neoprene is notorious for this, although some horses do very well with a neoprene mesh pad.

A saddle pad can "shim" a saddle with a somewhat less than perfect fit by adding filler material made of foam, gel, or neoprene. Be aware that adding more pad underneath a saddle that is too tight will *not* fix the saddle fit problem. Like wearing thick socks inside tight shoes, shoving a large pad under a pinching saddle will make the fit worse, not better.

Bridles and other headgear

Bridles come in an infinite variety. As always, style is optional but fit is essential. If you spend a lot of time riding in bad weather, synthetic tack may be a smart alternative to traditional leather.

Endurance headgear comes in a wide variety of colors and styles.

Nylon tack has been available for years. It is inexpensive and lasts a long time without tearing, stretching, or breaking. Many local feed stores carry basic nylon headgear, and most online tack stores sell nylon bridles and other nylon gear.

Many endurance riders prefer bridles and other tack pieces made from biothane or beta biothane, synthetic polyvinyl-coated polyester webbing. Biothane is more expensive than nylon, but it doesn't stretch, tear, break, or wear out even with years of heavy use in horrible weather. Beta biothane feels like good-quality leather. You will probably have to order biothane tack from an endurance vendor. (A list of endurance tack vendors is provided at the back of the book.)

Biothane and beta biothane tack require minimal effort to clean. I wash mine on the top rack of the dishwasher, but you can also toss biothane tack into a bucket of soapy water and rinse it off when you remember where you left it. An additional appeal is that it is available in a wide variety of colors: in addition to traditional brown or black, you can have a bridle that is bright red, neon or forest green, shiny white, sparkling blue, matte lilac, and many other colors. There are even glow-in-the-dark biothane materials available.

Bits

Ask a hundred riders which bit to use, and you will get more than a hundred different answers.

Ideally, choose a bit that gives you plenty of control over your horse during the excitement of a crowded start line, and one that will not hinder his ability to move freely down the trail.

In some cases, a single bit won't allow you to do both. Horses at the start line of a ride are often more "forward" (or "knuckleheaded") than normal; you may therefore wish to begin with a strong bit and change to a milder bit later in the day when your horse's demeanor has calmed down.

Breast collars, cruppers, martingales, tie-downs

I recommend using only the tack you need to use. If your horse doesn't need a martingale, leave it at home. If he has withers like a dorsal fin, you might be able to work without a crupper. If you don't do a lot of hill work, think about skipping the breast collar. The same goes for tie-downs, interference boots, and all other gadgetry. Use what you need; don't bother with anything else.

Saddle packs and bags

Endurance tack is often specifically engineered to minimize "bounce," but the same performance can often be achieved with computer-cable ties or adjustable dog collars wrapped around packs. Consider what you already have before spending money on the shiny stuff in the tack catalog. And if you like to have a designated place to stuff a jacket, a flashlight, or a granola bar, you can easily find saddle bags that will accommodate you.

A pack should be as waterproof as possible (alternately, use a trash bag tucked inside the pack to serve as a waterproof layer) and have the capacity to carry sufficient water for the rider for the day, as well as a little extra room for a carrot or two for your equine friend. You may also wish to carry a water bottle or two to squirt on your horse's neck for cooling. Don't forget which bottle is for cooling and which bottle is for drinking, especially if you plan to refill the cooling bottle out of a puddle or stock tank! We will discuss more details about cooling strategies for your horse in Chapter 11.

Horse shoes, bare feet, boots, and beyond

AERC has no specific requirements or restrictions regarding hoof protection during competition; as with so many other aspects of the sport, decisions about equine foot care are left to the owner and rider. A ride manager (RM) *is* permitted to require hoof protection for a specific ride, and some managers exercise that authority if they know that the footing on their ride is particularly rocky. In any case, RMs often *recommend* hoof protection for hard-terrain rides, rather than requiring that horses be shod or booted.

Four different hoof protection options (clockwise from top left): Renegade™ glue-on boots; Easy Boot™ glue-ons, traditional steel shoes, and Epona™ shoes (steel-reinforced plastic).

Although there are a variety of options, simple is often best. Shoeing is one place cutting corners does not pay off. A horse travels long distances in training and competition—it only makes sense to pay special attention to his foot care. Do not bring your horse to an event with 9-week-old shoes that are overgrown and barely tacked on! Savvy competitors will have their horse shod within a week or two of a ride's start.

If your horse needs an alternative to steel, consider urethane shoes, such as Ground Control™ horseshoes, or glue-on shoes. You may also wish to add plastic pads to the shoes of your horse if you train or compete on rocky terrain. These cushion the foot and provide protection from sharp rocks that can cause foot bruising and abscessing. Tender-footed horses may need pads for all terrains.

While endurance horses have traditionally been steel shod, the trend towards barefoot or barefoot-and-booted horses is growing, especially in dry climates like the American West. Karen Chaton, an early adopter of hoof boots, has ridden her horse Granite Chief more than 10,000 miles in competition for more than 6 years using boots over bare feet, and was the top mileage rider (on Chief and another barefoot/booted horse) in the 2011 Pony Express ride, a two month, multi-day ride covering 2,000 miles of the former Pony Express trail. Barefoot horses can do endurance when their feet are managed properly.

Choose a hoof management and protection strategy that suits your horse, your budget, and the terrain where you ride. Be proactive. Ask questions of your hoof care provider, your vet, and other distance riders in your region to find a strategy that works well for you and your horse.

Evaluating your tack

When evaluating your tack for endurance, ask yourself three questions:

- Does it fit?
- Is it safe?
- Is it comfortable?

Does it fit? If your horse has sores or tender spots from his tack, or if his hair grows in white where equipment has rubbed on him, it doesn't fit.

You may be able to change it, shim it, carve away bits, lengthen or shorten things, but do not ask your horse to travel long distances in ill-fitting gear. If you had a rock in your shoe, you would stop to fix the problem rather than leave the rock there for a few months hoping you'd get used to the pain.

Some thin-skinned horses will chafe more easily than their thicker-skinned cousins, especially in the girth or "armpit" region and under the gaiters of hoof boots. Using a layer of protective ointment like Desitin® may help; alternately, you may want to apply a lubricating substance like petroleum jelly or one of the countless slippery substances used by long-distance bicyclists (such as BodyGlide®; check with an outdoor or bicycling supply catalog for others). Easily-galled horses may require a smear of Desitin® as a preventative treatment.

Is it safe? If the leather is stretching, if the nylon is frayed, if the squeaking sound is getting louder, fix it *now*, before you or your horse gets hurt.

Check your tack frequently, especially the leather parts. Replace or repair worn tack before an unexpected stress causes your girth to snap, your bridle to break, or your stirrup to fall off. I have seen *all* of these potentially dangerous events occur on training rides and in competition, and each could have been prevented by a bit of proactive tack maintenance.

Is it comfortable? If there's a saddle concho that bumps your leg when you post, change it *now*. Likewise, if your stirrups seem a notch too short, *now* is a good time to adjust them. If there is a buckle that rubs your horse's skin, do him a favor and switch out the rigging *now*. There is nothing down the trail that will make a small annoyance smaller.

Other considerations. Here are a few other questions to ask yourself about your existing tack. While not as vital as those listed above, these are also important.

Is this equipment sturdy enough to last for many years? When a good piece of tack begins to show wear, find a way to replace it with something that will serve you as well or better. High quality tack can last your lifetime if you care for it.

Does this tack require a lot of time to keep it clean? Can I replace it with something that will work well but not need so much maintenance? Nobody *needs* biothane tack… but if you ride in unfriendly weather, you might spend a lot of time cleaning your leather tack, when you might be happier spending that time riding your horse.

If your tack fits properly but your horse still shows soreness (especially in his back), consider asking a trainer to evaluate the way you ride. Better riding technique helps the horse move with greater ease and comfort, especially as both of you get tired.

Clothing for the rider

With the exception of a helmet requirement for junior riders, the AERC is silent on the matter of rider apparel. As far as the rules are concerned, you can show up wearing nothing but a smile. However, there are a few items of clothing that you may want to consider.

Helmet

The AERC requires helmets for only junior riders. Many adult endurance riders won't get in the saddle without one, however. A helmet is the single most important piece of equipment for keeping you safe.

The American Academy of Pediatrics, the American Medical Association through the Committee on Sports Medicine, the Canadian Medical Association, and the American Medical Equestrian Association/Safe Riders Foundation (now the EMSA) recommend that approved, fitted, and secured helmets be worn on all rides by all horseback riders.

2.2: A few facts about equestrian helmets

A few facts about helmets, courtesy of the Equestrian Medical Safety Association (http://www.emsaonline.net/helmet_safety.html):

- Approximately 20% of horse-related injuries occur on the ground, not while riding.
- Most riding injuries occur during pleasure riding.
- Among riders, the most common injuries that result in hospital admission and death are head injuries.
- A fall from 2 feet (60 cm) can cause permanent brain damage. A horse elevates a rider 8 feet (3 meters) or more above ground.
- A human skull can be shattered by an impact of 7-10 kph. Horses can gallop at 65 kph.
- A rider who has one head injury has a 40% chance of suffering a second head injury. Children, teens, and young adults are most vulnerable to sudden death from second impact syndrome (severe brain swelling that results from suffering a second head injury before recovering from the first head injury).
- Death is not the only serious outcome of unprotected head injuries. Those who survive with brain injury may suffer epilepsy, intellectual and memory impairment, and personality changes.
- Hospital costs for an acute head injury can be in the range of $25,000 per day. Lifetime extended-care costs may easily exceed $3 million. There is no funding for rehabilitation outside the medical setting.
- *Helmets work.* Most deaths from head injury can be prevented by wearing ASTM- (American Society for Testing Materials) or SEI- (Safety Equipment Institute) approved helmets that fit correctly and have the harness firmly applied. Other types of helmets, including bike helmets, are inadequate.

Don't forget your helmet!

If you are disinclined to wear a helmet even after reading the statistics, I recommend that you view the YouTube video featuring former USET rider Courtney King Dye speaking about her 2010 helmetless ride and accident that resulted in a traumatic brain injury. The link to this video and other informational online videos available are listed in the "Useful Links and Resources" appendix at the back of this book.

My final word on the topic of helmets: *If you think your hairstyle is more important than your brains, you are probably right.*

Jeans, breeches, or tights?

Many riders new to endurance are a bit shy about pulling on brightly-colored tights. If so, jeans are perfectly acceptable as ride-day apparel; however, you may want to minimize chafing by choosing jeans with no inner-leg seam. An old cowboy secret to avoid clothing burns is to wear pantyhose under the blue jeans; long underwear can serve the same function and will also keep your bum warm on a cold day.

English riding breeches are another popular choice. Breeches allow more movement than blue jeans, which may be helpful if you are crawling aboard an especially tall horse. Men who are shy about buying breeches may find that baseball pants are pretty much the same garment and work just as well.

Then, of course, there are the tights in unusual colors and patterns. Riding tights may also feature knee padding and/or padding in the crotch and bum areas, welcome features for riders who cover a lot of miles in a single day.

Rain gear

Even if you live in a warm, dry climate, you should be prepared for weather to roll in on an endurance ride. A good quality water*proof* (not water-*resistant*) jacket or poncho can make the difference between a pleasant ride and a cold, wet, miserable day on the trail. In the rainy climate where I live, Gore-Tex™ is the waterproof, breathable fabric of choice.

Many riders use rain pants in addition to a waterproof jacket; others prefer a long, Aussie-style drover's coat made of waxed cotton or oilcloth that covers the rider's entire body from chin to ankles. "Rain chinks" made of Gore-Tex™ and fleece are a relatively new option that strap around the rider's waist and cover the upper thigh and knees, affording a warming, water-shedding layer that is less restrictive than rain pants or a long coat.

No matter what you use for rain gear, be sure to test-ride it before a ride day, or risk getting wet if the fit isn't quite right.

These rain chinks can be removed while the rider is still in the saddle.

Warm gear for cold weather

The most important clothing rule to remember for cold and wet weather riding is that *cotton kills.*

The wonderful, cooling property of cotton fabric that makes it so welcome on hot, humid days can make it a deadly contributor to hypothermia in cold and wet weather. Water-soaked cotton clothing provides no insulation and does not wick moisture away from the skin. Even if the air temperature is above freezing, if it is colder than your body temperature, wet cotton clothing will chill you. Keep in mind that cotton clothing might also be called corduroy, denim, flannel, or duck—avoid these fabrics if there is any possibility of precipitation or cold temperatures when you are riding. This includes undergarments. Stick with synthetic or silk and stay warm!

Layering your clothing is an excellent strategy to stay comfortable during cold weather. Start with synthetic, silk, or wool undergarments and socks. Some riders prefer natural fibers like wool and silk for middle layers, others swear by high-tech fabrics like fleece. Gloves and a helmet liner also help retain body heat, and a wind-proof, waterproof outer layer can always be removed if the weather is clear or warmer than anticipated.

Keep in mind that your body will often stay warm while you are moving down the trail at a trot, but if you slow or stop, you can become chilled quickly. Consider carrying an extra layer of warm clothing tied to your saddle as a precaution. Chemical hand- and foot-warmers are small, lightweight, and easily stashed in pockets or packs if extra warming is needed.

REI and other outdoor gear suppliers are good places to shop for clothing, especially outerwear. However, don't expect the clerk at Cabala's to understand what it means to ride all day. The gear clerk who has heard of our sport is rare and valuable. A better bet is to tell a clerk that you will be out hiking in potentially inclement weather… for a week.

Don't forget Army/Navy surplus stores and thrift shops as you search. These generally won't carry endurance-specific gear such as tights with knee padding, but they often have a wide selection of rain gear, synthetic fleece, and wool clothing.

Cool gear for hot weather

Riding in extreme heat can also be hazardous for an unprepared rider. Riding in hot, direct sunlight can lead to heat illness or heat stroke—a medical emergency—especially if there is no shade where you can rest. The clothing you take with you on the trail can make a huge difference.

When riding in hot weather, your t-shirt may feel fine; however, doctors recommend that that you minimize harmful exposure to UVR (ultraviolet rays) by doing the following:

Apply sunscreen. If your skin is fair, carry some with you on the trail and re-apply frequently.

Stay in the shade as much as possible. This, unfortunately, isn't always an option during endurance training or competition; however, when you stop on the trail or at the vet check, take advantage of any available shade to rest in.

Cover up with clothes. A white cotton t-shirt is the equivalent of a coating of SPF-5 sunscreen. Tightly woven fabrics of darker colors offer even more protection. High-tech SPF-enhanced clothing may be a good investment if you are prone to sunburn or heat injury.

Consider taking along a "top shirt" which can be dunked in a creek, a puddle, or a water tank, or squirted with water from your water bottle before you put it on. A wide-brimmed visor designed to attach to your helmet is a handy accessory that will keep direct sunlight off your face. (It will also keep raindrops from smearing your glasses if you wear them!) I wear a silk bandana over my head and under my helmet year-round. It keeps my head warmer in winter, and prevents strange-looking sunburn on my scalp from the helmet vent holes in summer. The bandanna can also be dunked in water, then secured under the helmet for a bit of cool refreshment on hot days.

With no shade in sight, smart riders cover up with clothing.

Heat protective garments such as cooling vests and cooling helmet liners—there are even cooling bra inserts—may be a good investment if you are sensitive to high temperatures and/or high humidity.

Footwear

The traditional "boot with a heel" is always a good choice, but if you ride with caged stirrups you may prefer riding with sneakers, running shoes, or even hiking boots. If you like to walk or run alongside your horse, choose shoes or boots with good traction for the terrain. If you ride with smaller or English-style stirrup irons, be sure that your boot isn't so snug in the stirrup that it can get stuck and create a hazardous situation if you need to dismount swiftly.

Your goal in choosing appropriate footgear is the same as your goal in choosing other riding gear mentioned in this section—to find something that fits and is comfortable for you and for your style of riding.

Foundation and support garments

Women. The highly-valued springy, floating trot exhibited by certain breeds of endurance horses has an unfortunate effect on generously endowed women. And let's face it—bouncing boobs are no fun to experience for 25 miles or more. So, what's a girl to do for her… girlz?

Here are some recommendations for making it work, gleaned from personal experience and the Ridecamp listserv (www.endurance.net/ridecamp), where the topic is discussed at least once a year:

- Wear a properly fitting bra;
- TWO properly fitting bras, one on top of the other;
- Duct tape or medical tape under the straps (to avoid chafing); or
- A bra made from a technical wicking fabric.

Note: Custom-made bras may be more expensive than an off-the-shelf model, but *worth it* if you are size D or larger.

Men. Although logic would dictate that sensible (and sensitive) men ride sidesaddle, tradition dictates that they straddle the saddle just like sensible women. To avoid diminishment of the family jewels, here are some recommendations gleaned from riders in my own ridecamp as well as the Ridecamp listserv (www.endurance.net/ridecamp):

- Wear compression shorts, such as Under Armour®;
- Flat-seamed wicking-fabric briefs;
- Pantyhose (worn under jeans or riding tights, not on top);
- Padded breeches;
- Padded bicycle shorts worn beneath breeches or tights;
- Tights or breeches designed for men;
- Tights or breeches NOT designed for men; or
- Baseball pants, sweats, or yoga pants.

2.3: Is the clothing you already have suitable?

Does it fit?

Is it safe?

Is it comfortable?

Do you have enough freedom of movement to mount your horse or perform an emergency dismount?

Does it offer protection from weather, helping you stay cool on hot days or warm on cold days?

Can you easily and conveniently add or remove layers while still mounted?

Both Genders. No matter what you wear, you may experience chafing or fabric burns from your clothing over the course of a long day in the saddle. Here are some solutions to consider:

A "seat saver" can add miles of comfort. Some riders prefer a sheepskin that covers the saddle seat and the stirrup leathers; others are more comfortable with a gel-filled pad that cushions only the seat of the saddle. Real sheepskin is more expensive than acrylic fleece, but will not cause friction burns. Experiment to find the material and style that suits you best.

Smear lubricating creams (such as BodyGlide®, sold to long-distance bicyclists) on legs, under bra straps, beneath waistbands, and any other place that clothing tends to rub. For best results, do this *the night before the ride,* and then (without washing the first layer off) re-apply in the morning. As one rider told me, you will only forget to do this once.

Liberally dust Gold Bond powder, baby powder, or finely-powdered cornstarch over the parts of you that tend to sweat and then chafe.

Take a change of clothing for part-way through the event. If you bring only one spare garment, make it socks!

If chafing has already occurred and your day isn't finished yet, zinc oxide (Desitin®) or any other baby ointment will protect the spot from further damage, even in intimate personal locations.

Fanny packs and pockets: What to put in them

A fanny pack is a handy place to store most of the stuff—including that Gold Bond powder and extra socks—recommended for all hikers and riders in the wilderness. The Mountaineers, a group of highly skilled outdoor recreation enthusiasts and educators, recommend carrying at least "The 10 Essentials."

2.4: The Mountaineers' "10 Essential [Survival] Systems"

1) Navigation (map & compass)
2) Sun protection (sunglasses & sunscreen)
3) Insulation (extra clothing)
4) Illumination (headlamp/flashlight)
5) First aid supplies
6) Fire (waterproof matches/lighter/candle)
7) Repair kit and tools
8) Nutrition (extra food)
9) Hydration (extra water)
10) Emergency shelter (tent/plastic tube tent/garbage bag)

You might think that hauling around the 10 Essentials is a bit of overkill—after all, you will be participating in an organized event, on a marked trail. However, STUFF HAPPENS. You may never need any of the Essentials (except the sunscreen). But then again, you might. If you or someone travelling with you becomes sick or injured, or if you get off trail (more about that in Chapter 13), you may need to build a fire or set up a temporary shelter under a garbage bag. There may come a day when you are glad of a pack of matches, an extra granola bar, a trash bag, and some duct tape.

I recommend that riders also carry Benadryl tablets with them. Insect bites or stings are annoying most of the time, but occasionally a bite or sting may trigger a dangerous allergic reaction. If you encounter bees, hornets, yellow jackets or any of their kin on the trail, a dose of Benadryl might save your life or the life of a riding partner.

What it comes down to is this

If your saddle fits you properly, if your clothes fit you properly, if you're properly prepared, and you *still* experience significant pain from rubbing or chafing, consider taking some riding lessons. A good instructor can teach you techniques to carry yourself down the trail more gently.

The Bad Idea Fairy has a tack sale

For Sale — Make an offer:

BigName Fancy Saddle: Lots of silver, looks awesome. Fits any horse. It only looks like the tree is broken. I'm selling because my horse bucks when he wears it.

BigHonkin Bit: Lots of "whoa." I didn't have time to clean the bloodstains off.

Interference Boots: Everybody uses them; you should too.

Helmet: Only one dent. Super cheap!

Your horse's pulse will drop when he lowers his head. Sirie Neal Michaels has taught Arianna to do this on cue.

CHAPTER 3
BEGINNING THE TRAINING AT HOME

Training for an endurance event can be a lot like eating an elephant: The task is absolutely impossible unless you take it one small bite at a time. The trick is to figure out where to start.

In this chapter, you'll see a lot of lists. The first list is really important stuff you probably already know how to do if you've ridden your horse in any other discipline, from trail riding to stadium jumping. At the end of it there's a new skill to learn that is peculiar to endurance competitions: the trot-out. Next comes a list of skills that are a little out of the ordinary—not absolutely essential, but good to practice. Finally, there's a list of crazy but potentially useful exercises that can be fun for you and your horse.

What the horse and rider should already know

Endurance riders often come to the sport from other disciplines and should therefore already have basic (or advanced) skills in the saddle. If you and your horse have these skills already, proceed to the next section. If you and your horse need practice in the following skills, move them to the top of your priority list.

Walk/trot/canter under saddle. Easy-gaited horses should be able to perform their specialty gaits on cue.

Steer. Endurance trails often aren't straight. Sometimes they are built over trails pounded into the dirt by mountain bikers, or dogsled teams, or even the most capricious animals on earth: elk. Practice tight turns slowly before adding speed.

Stop. If your horse has no brakes, get busy and install them. On the trail things sometimes happen with little warning and you will want to be able to *whoa* when you need to *whoa*. In my community, 4-H kids teach their mounts to stop from a walk/trot/canter or gallop when the rider drops both stirrups. You may never need such extreme skills, but it doesn't hurt to practice them. If your horse won't GO, you can call a trainer to help fix the problem, but if your horse won't STOP, you may have to call an ambulance.

Skills to practice for success

Don't feel badly if your horse doesn't do a lot of the things listed in the next section. I competed for many years on a horse who wouldn't allow himself to be caught promptly in a pasture, who couldn't be trusted inside an electric corral, and whose idea of "rating" consisted of pulling my arms out of the socket for the first 60 miles before trotting on a loose rein for the rest of the day—unless he saw a scary cow… or a scary leaf… which prompted a sudden swoop to the left. I completed a lot of miles with him, but I knew he was missing skills that would make my life easier. At that time, though, I lacked the knowledge and support to teach them.

The following list is meant to be a starting point. If there's one thing that endurance riders have a lot of, it's time. Use your time to improve your horse's training in ways that will make your life easier whether you're at home, on the trail, or at camp. If a horse can be taught the following skills, it will also make his experience better.

The rider should stay on the same side of the horse as the vet during an exam.

At home

Eat with enthusiasm. I'm not sure you can teach this to a horse, but you'll find that finicky eaters can be incredibly frustrating on the trail. Learn your horse's food preference. Is he a hay eater? A beet pulp fanatic? Does he prefer carrots over apples?

If your horse is a picky eater even when he is thin and/or working hard and the feed is accepted by others in the herd, ask your vet's advice. Blood work, dental work, or endoscopy may find something that, when remedied, will make your horse eat... well... like a horse!

Wait patiently for food without running over the person carrying the feed buckets. Horses get hungry when they are working hard, but they still need to mind their manners. My food-motivated mare is required to stay three steps away from the feed pan until I say "okay." A less pushy horse won't need this practice.

Stand to be caught and haltered; walk calmly on a lead. Practice, practice, practice. It may be convenient for you to open a stall door and release him into a pasture at home, but if your horse doesn't walk politely on a lead rope, consider moving him from place to place on a lead every day for a few months. When the skill becomes routine, you will be glad you spent those extra minutes practicing.

Stand still for brushing, tacking up, de-worming, and other routine activities, and stand quietly while blankets, sheets and tack are taken on and off. Endurance horses get fiddled with a lot, often by strangers. If your horse is goosey, wiggly, or impatient, teach him to stand quietly as you do routine stuff around him.

During a competition, your horse may be examined or handled by 10 or more people in a single day, so prepare him by recruiting people he doesn't know well to pick up his feet, apply a stethoscope, draw numbers on his bum (I use my knuckle for practice, it feels the same to the horse), poke at his gums, and sponge him with water.

Load into the trailer promptly, ride without fussing, and unload quietly. Again, practice is essential. If your horse is a reluctant loader, consider feeding him all his meals inside the trailer for a month or two. If he is a fussy traveler, borrow a calm "teaching" horse to ride with him. Vary the length of your journeys, so that he doesn't come to expect a trip of a specific length and then grow anxious if you keep on driving. Put the loveliest hay you can find into a hay bag for him to snack on as he rides. When you stop for a break, offer carrots or apple slices.

Also, if your trailer is a slant load, borrow a straight load and practice getting your horse in and out of it. If it's a straight load, practice with a slant load. In an emergency evacuation, you do NOT want to discover that your horse is dangerously unprepared to load into a new type of trailer.

Practice *unloading* too. Practice until you and your horse are comfortable backing out of a straight load, turning around inside a slant load, stepping down from a step-up, or clomping down a ramp.

A nervous horse will be happier if he is tied next to a calm buddy.

At home and away, stand quietly while tied to a trailer or hitching post. You really want to know that the horse you tied to the trailer will still be there—standing calmly and not trying to commit suicide with the rope—when you return after leaving him for a few minutes (or longer). Practice tying him to the trailer for long periods only after he has mastered standing quietly while tied at home.

Accept being hobbled. In addition to enabling you to set your horse loose to graze in camp (if conditions allow), hobble practice is useful if a horse is caught in vines or wire: A hobble-trained horse will stand and wait to be freed from the entanglement and will not panic or thrash around.

On the trail

Walk flat-footed away from the trailer. Even if your horse practices this at home, he may still be light footed at the start line. And a horse that isn't required to walk calmly away from the trailer at home will *never* walk calmly to the start line of a ride in an exciting ridecamp.

Move down the trail at the gait and speed you request, extending or collecting as needed. This is called "rating." Here's where arena practice will help: rehearse your communication and balance skills in a flat, controlled space without any strange obstacles to distract you, and then apply those skills on the trail whenever you encounter changes in terrain and footing.

For rating practice at the trot, for example, choose landmarks within the arena. Pillars or wall studs are good for this, or you can set up traffic cones at regular intervals. Count the number of strides between markers, then try to increase the number of strides between them. Next time, try decreasing the number of strides without changing speed. Then practice increasing the speed *without* increasing the number of strides.

Teach your horse to save energy by keeping in gait while adjusting the length and speed of the stride with minimal cues from the rider. The goal is to be able to slow him down without having to yank on his face or run him into a tree. Practice by varying your routine—if you always canter up a particular hill, periodically walk up it instead.

Step or hop over fallen logs. Practice this at home using cavalletti, ground poles, or clean lumber as obstacles for the horse to navigate over. Once he can easily manage this, place them at weird angles, stack them strangely, or cross them from different directions.

Tread carefully through rocky areas and on slippery, muddy terrain, and choose good footing when it's available. Some horses seem to do this instinctively; others learn by watching more experienced horses. If necessary, hop down from the saddle and lead your horse on foot, asking him to follow in your footsteps through brushy or otherwise iffy terrain. The ideal endurance trail is free of rocks, brush, and other barriers, but I rarely see trails like that. With practice, your horse will learn to choose the best footing available on the trail. I sometimes train in areas that are professionally logged, a process that leaves a bizarre tangle of debris atop the trails; because of this practice, my mare has become quite competent at picking her way through branches without worry.

Cross water without incident. Horses don't have the same kind of depth perception that humans have; to their eyes, an ordinary mud puddle might look like a bottomless alligator pit. Practice crossing as many kinds of water as you can find: clear puddles, murky puddles, running creeks, etc. If you live in an arid climate, practice walking over tarps to partially re-create the experience of water underfoot.

When riding with a group of horses, take the lead position, the tail position, or the middle position. Many horses have a preferred "marching order"; however, you may not always be able to give your horse his preference. Teach him to accept various places within a travelling group by trading positions during each ride with your riding partners.

Leave a group of horses and move down the trail without them. This can be hard for herd-bound horses. With such a horse, practice separating from a group in slow stages. At first you may only be able to walk him to the far side of a tree. Gradually lengthen the separations until you can safely leave the group or be left behind by them. And you can combine herd-bound training with rating training by asking the horse to change his speed or the length of his stride while in a group, creating more space between him and the other horses. With anxious horses, approach this change slowly until they gain confidence.

Water crossings are common at endurance events.

Move down the trail solo. Some horses prefer going solo. These horses are happier when allowed to leave the group. But for others, this is sometimes very difficult. Be sure to practice both solo work *and* group riding.

Allow other horses to pass on the trail. A few horses become anxious when other horses pass them on the trail; others become aggressive. Know your horse's tendencies and work on getting him to move forward politely and calmly as other horses move around you. If your horse is a kicker, flag his tail with a red ribbon so that considerate riders can give lots of room between the horses.

Pass other horses on the trail without incident or misbehavior. A horse may also become anxious or aggressive when passing other horses. Practice until you are confident that he will behave properly, and if in doubt, flag your horse's tail with red ribbon.

Grab bites of grass when directed to do so by the rider. In stark contrast to everything we learned in 4-H and Pony Club, endurance riders encourage their horses to eat along the trail *when directed* to do so.

3.1 Eating on the trail (how *not* to do it)

Don't make the mistake a friend of mine made by allowing her mare to grab bites of food any old time, or you may find yourself sailing over your horse's head when he slams on his brakes to grab a bite of grass between his feet. I use the verbal cue "Oh look: food" when I want my mount to turn to the side of the trail and take a few bites of grass. It's a stupid command, but my horses all know what it means: we won't be moving forward until their mouths are full.

Drink out of buckets, streams, puddles, or a helmet. A normally fastidious horse will learn this skill quickly if he gets thirsty. To encourage a reluctant horse to drink, administer a dose of electrolytes at the beginning of the workout session, and when you suspect that he's thirsty, offer him water from a puddle. He'll figure it out.

Take treats politely from your hand while you are mounted. This is a convenient way to allow your horse a snack of carrots or apples on a long ride, especially on terrain that offers minimal forage. Experienced riders are able to administer electrolytes from the saddle, and I know one mare that will drink Snapple out of a bottle held in the mounted rider's hand.

Stand quietly while the rider chats with other riders, checks the map, fixes helmet straps or unwraps a sandwich.

Stand quietly when the rider is dismounted and remain standing quietly to allow the rider to remount. There is nothing more distracting than having a horse use you as a maypole when you're trying to pee by the side of the trail. Practice this!

Look who's taller now!

I am short and my horse is tall, so I've taught her to sidle up to any stump, rock, or random pickup truck that I can use as a mounting block. She allows herself to be placed in a ditch if that's the only low ground I can find. And I've taught her to stretch out one or both of her front legs on command, an action which drops her back down by about 2 inches, making mounting from the ground possible for me.

Transition between activities smoothly and without debate. Practice trotting down the trail, and then stopping for a bite of grass, followed by more trotting. Practice walking, dismounting, remounting, and then walking again. Your horse will learn that he may be asked to change activities at any time. Do some bending practice, or work on laterals while you're on the trail. This will keep his mind engaged, and his body limber.

In camp

Stay within his corral or on his tie without fussing. If your horse is extremely anxious when you arrive at your first ridecamp, be prepared to sit beside his enclosure with a nice paperback book. This allows him to see that you are present and not worried about your surroundings. If possible, bring an experienced "buddy horse" to give a worried horse some company and guidance on his first trips to camp.

Eat, drink, and observe camp activity without undue concern or worry. Again, this comes with practice. Know what works to calm or distract your horse. A food-motivated horse will be more interested in the lovely hay and beet pulp you have given him than in the monsters lurking in the bushes. A friend-motivated horse will copy the behavior of buddies standing nearby, so try to camp beside horses who are calm and quiet.

If you are worried that your horse may try to escape during the night, tie him to the trailer with two lead ropes, one longer and one shorter. He might break the first one, but you will (hopefully) hear the commotion and leap up to intervene before he breaks the second one.

Notice the repetition in this list—words and phrases like "stand quietly," for example. Also, "without fussing."

Endurance horses need to conserve strength for the trail and not waste your time and their own energy by being knuckleheaded during absolutely routine activities. For many horses, this is easy; for others, it can be an enormous challenge. Practice will help.

Teaching the trot-out

The trot-out is an exercise used by endurance riders and veterinarians to evaluate the soundness, fitness, and attitude of a horse. If your horse is easy gaited, follow the instructions given for trotting horses and cue your horse to perform his own specialty gait.

Seasoned competitors make a trot-out look easy. The rider skims along the ground beside a springy, well-behaved horse, travelling in a straight line away from the vet for 100 to 125 feet, slowing to walk around a traffic cone at the far end, and then trotting back to the vet without stumbling, crowding, wandering out of the lane, or running out of steam on the return journey.

Experienced endurance teams make the trot-out look easy.

The vet watches the horse's movement and attitude during the trot-out to determine the presence or absence of lameness and the quality of the movement. A sound horse will move off with a steady, rhythmic gait which looks and sounds symmetric to the observer. A fresh horse moves out eagerly, with attention to his handler on the ground.

Ideally, you want to start with a horse that walks properly on a lead line: his head stays even with your shoulder; the lead line is looped between you, not tight like a kite string. When you walk, he walks. When you stop, he stops. When you turn, he turns.

Below are some tips for teaching a horse how to trot-out for the vet.

The departure. You and your horse are standing still, facing the same directions.

Jiggle the lead rope a little, and say in your perkiest voice, "Ready?"

Wait for a count of two, and then stride off briskly.

Ideally, your horse will stride off briskly beside you. Repeat the exercise at the trot. Your horse should jog along beside you on a loose line. If he does, hurray! Skip to the section labeled "The turn." If he doesn't, keep reading.

Your horse may be a Ferdinand who would rather sit and sniff the flowers than move forward properly on the line. If you have a Ferdinand, pick up a dressage or longe whip with your left hand, and hold the lead rope in your right hand. If you don't have a longe whip, a slender, springy branch from a tree will do. You want something lightweight that will reach from the outside of your body to the back end of your horse when you are standing beside him. Practice the reach while you are standing still beside your horse so that you can learn exactly how it feels.

Now, try this:

You and Ferdinand are standing still, facing the same direction.

Jiggle the lead rope a little, and say "Ready?"

Trot off briskly away from the vet.

Wait for a count of two, and then stride off briskly in a fast walk *and simultaneously reach back with your stick or whip and **ping** Ferdinand on the bum.*

You know your horse, and you know how reactive he is. If he's extremely sensitive, a little ping on the bum will make him leap forward to join you. If he does this, *praise him* and keep moving forward for about 5 or 6 strides.

Then, slow for 5 or 6 strides. Halt. Repeat the start with standing still, rope jiggle, and verbal cue "Ready?"

If your Ferdinand is as sensitive as a stump, enlist the help of a friend who will also be armed with a whip or tree branch. Put your friend on the other side of Ferdinand, beside his right hip, but out of the reach of a kicking leg. Begin the process again.

You and Ferdinand are standing still, facing the same direction.

Jiggle the lead rope a little, and say "Ready?"

Wait for a count of two, and then stride off briskly in a fast walk and simultaneously reach back with your stick and ping Ferdinand on the bum *while your friend simultaneously whomps Ferdinand on the bum from the other side.*

As soon as Ferdinand moves forward (even if he leaps forward in surprise), *praise him* and keep moving forward for 5 or 6 strides. Then, slow for 5 or 6 strides. Halt. Allow your friend to rejoin you, and repeat the process.

With repetition, Ferdinand will learn that the rope jiggle and verbal "Ready?" are his cue that in a moment or two, he will be asked to move out to avoid whompage. You can gradually ease off on your whomping: your friend's help will become unnecessary, and eventually you won't need a whip in your own hand to get Ferdinand to move out. He will be watching you and waiting for the rope jiggle and verbal cue.

When Ferdinand is proficient at the brisk walk, practice the same exercise at a slow trot.

The turn. Some people prefer to trot around the turn, but I like to have my horse trot out to the marker, walk around the turn, and then trot back to the vet. As we get to the cone, I will jiggle the lead rope and say, "a-a-a-and Walk," as I slow my stride.

Ideally, the horse will match my speed as I slow, and will walk politely around the outside of me as I walk around the outside of the cone. If your horse does this, hurray! Skip down to the section "The return."

If your horse is a Freight Train and it's hard to get him to slow down, keep reading.

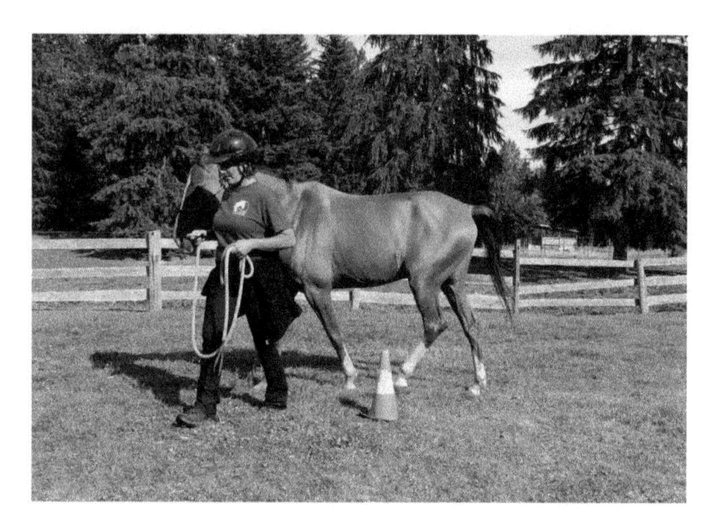

Walk in a wide circle around the cone.

Start this practice at a very brisk walk. When you get better at it, practice at a trot. Take your dressage whip or a slender tree branch with you.

You and Freight Train stride along briskly, side by side.

You jiggle the lead rope a little and say, "a-a-a-nd Walk" as you slow your stride. This is his cue that you will be slowing down.

Reach in front of your own body and Freight Train's chest with your whip, and push on him. If he is a sensitive soul, a little tap is all it will take, but if necessary, push hard. You may want to give a correction "pop" with the lead rope at the same time. Do whatever it takes to get Freight Train to check his speed for a stride or two.

As soon as he slows, *praise him and change directions, executing a sharp turn to the left away from him, and walking slower but not stopping.*

Repeat the exercise. Move forward briskly; give Freight Train the rope jiggle and verbal cue "a-a-a-and Walk" as you slow your stride. As soon as he hesitates or slows, praise him and change directions at a slower pace.

Randomly change the direction of your turn: turn left, turn right, turn at strange angles, do the hokey pokey and turn yourself around.

Once he's paying close attention, turn so that you walk right in front of your Train, so that he must slam on the brakes and turn on his haunches to avoid walking on top of you. Freight Train will learn that the rope jiggle and verbal command to walk are his cue to slow down and prepare to change directions.

The return. You and your horse are executing the turn around a traffic cone at a controlled walk. As you come back around to face the way you came, jiggle the rope, give the verbal cue, and pick up the speed again.

If your horse is a Ferdinand, you want the return pace to be *brisk*.

If your horse is a Freight Train, practice controlling his speed.

Go for the speed and control you want a few strides at a time. If your horse can do something successfully for 5 strides, with more practice he will do it for 15 strides, and from there he can do it for the 100 feet from the cone to the vet.

The halt. Ferdinand will soon learn that the vet is the ultimate destination of this exercise, and that when you get to the vet, you will halt. Ferdinand likes to stand still, so he will try to halt early... then earlier and earlier... until the unprepared rider finds herself dragging an unwilling, joint-locked beast for the final 20 strides.

To avoid this situation, choose a spot about 3 strides in front of the vet and be ready to give the cue "a-a-a-and Walk" when you get to that spot *and not a single stride earlier.* You may have to carry your whip to enforce this idea. You might also throw a handful of tasty hay at the vet's feet... and make sure that Ferdinand sees it before you leave on your trot to the cone. He won't forget it's there and he'll be eager to return to it.

Freight Train presents the opposite problem: he likes to accelerate during the trot-out, even (or especially) when the rider can't keep up. Practice frequent stops, turns, and slowdowns with Freight Train, so that he learns to watch and listen to his handler during the trot-out. If he thinks you might just halt and turn and point him a random direction midway, he's less likely to charge forward full blast.

Walk the final three strides and halt with the horse (not the handler) standing squarely in front of the vet.

With both Ferdinand and Freight Train, it's important that your last 3 strides towards the vet be executed at a controlled walk to avoid alarming anybody. There is one vet on the endurance circuit who promises that if any horse runs over a vet, the vet's scribe, or the vet's truck, he will personally take the pulse of the ride manager and write *that* on the horse's ride card, ensuring a non-completion.

Rather than take the risk of injuring ride staff or any other bystanders, practice control in the final stage of the trot-out.

Note that when you come to a complete stop, the horse and not the handler should be standing directly in front of the vet.

Putting it all together. Enlist a friend to play the part of the vet for your practice session.

Before you begin, take a deep breath; think for a moment about the departure, the turn, the return, the halt, and how you plan to correct your horse's behavior if it needs to be corrected. Then exhale, take hold of the lead line, jiggle the rope, and begin.

Have your friend watch to make sure you are traveling in a straight line out and back, and shout encouragement or corrections as needed to keep you and your horse on course. It's important to note that the vet watching your trot-out is usually NOT looking at the horse's feet. Instead, the vet is watching for symmetry of movement in the shoulders and hips which indicates soundness, and is looking for a head bob which may indicate pain in one or more feet or limbs. To avoid having the handler drag the horse down by his face at any point during the exercise, practice until the trot-out can be done on a completely loose rein or lead line.

By taking time to teach your horse these steps *before* bringing him to camp, you are providing him with a useful skill that vets and volunteers will appreciate, and that will ensure that your horse is shown in the best possible way during his vet-check exams.

Surviving unusual stuff on the trail

To develop some of these skills, such as "navigate through bad terrain," a rider must deliberately seek out opportunities to practice. Most riders prefer to avoid slippery mud, steep uphills and downhills, sharp rocks, and trails covered by fallen trees, but you never know what you will encounter out on the trail, so practice crazy stuff, just in case. "Trust training" may be the most important tool in your bag if the world ever goes pear-shaped on the trail. A horse who has emotionally bonded with you will trust you to pull him out of situations that might seem (to him) to be crazy. See Sidebar 3.2 for an example.

Help your horse remain quiet and calm by keeping your own manner quiet and calm, your movements smooth and deliberate, and your voice low and friendly.

Practice calm, quiet behavior at home and in training to encourage similar behavior in a ridecamp and on the trail. Seek out challenging terrain, weird noises, and strange situations so that you and your horse can practice coping together.

Allow a young horse to satisfy his curiosity about unusual objects.

If you need additional help "bombproofing" your horse, contact a mounted horse police unit. Many of these conduct periodic bombproofing clinics for their members and interested civilians, teaching horses how to cope with gunfire, flashing lights and sirens, and a number of truly unusual situations.

3.2: The helicopter story

One day my horse and I were out solo. We headed to the top of the hill on an old logging road, where I planned to ride part of the ridge trail there and cut back down on another trail, through the neighbor's back yard and home again. It was an ordinary day and an ordinary ride on trails we use all the time.

I reckoned without the helicopter.

The contraption was parked at the top of the hill, in the middle of the trail. The engine was turned off, but the rotors were still spinning slowly, so I guessed it hadn't been parked there very long. The pilot was nowhere in sight.

My mare was, naturally, a little nonplussed. She had seen plenty of machines in her days on the racetrack, including trucks and tractors and starting gates and who knows what else. She'd seen plenty of stuff while travelling with me, including all the machinery associated with a working logging camp — bulldozers and boom rigs and semi-trucks and chainsaws.

But she'd never seen a helicopter on the trail before. How do you prepare your horse for something like that?

The answer, obviously, is that you *can't* train your horse to be helicopter safe, unless you have a helicopter handy for frequent practice sessions, which I didn't.

However, I had taken her into plenty of weird situations before we met the helicopter.

Early in our partnership, I got into the habit of riding into town (about 7 miles) to the little hamburger drive-in, where I ordered a cheeseburger for myself and some sugar packets for my horse.

She was a big hit with the restaurant staff and the customers, and the side benefit was that she learned to accept things like cars, traffic lights, and the sliding window at the drive-in.

Another time, we were up on top of Blanchard Mountain, and as usual, I knew only vaguely where we were (but I can always find my way home, which is an important skill). I didn't realize that the big open space we had found was a launching spot for the local hang gliders.

It wasn't exactly labeled "Hang Glider Crossing."

But there we were, munching our lunches, when *flappity-flappity-flappity,* along came a very nice fellow, lugging his brightly colored hang-glider wings.

I pulled a sugar packet out of my pocket and handed it to the nice fellow to feed to my mare. She saw the packet and forgave the fellow for his weird wings immediately. No problem.

So the day my horse and I met the helicopter, she wasn't worried about the machine.

Oh no.

She figured that anybody with a rig *that* weird looking was certain to have sugar packets.

She was hunting for the pilot.

Practice that can be done at home, without access to a trail

Below I list a few ideas for training to deal with obstacles. For additional ideas, take a look at the American Competitive Trail Horse Association website.

Bridges. Build a small "bridge" to practice with. It need not be more than 6 to12 inches tall or more than 8 to10 feet long. Teach your horse to cross on cue without hesitation. Don't trot or canter over the bridge—bridges become slippery with minute amounts of moisture, and you want your horse to approach them calmly and slowly.

Your practice bridge can be simple, or fancy like this one.

Drag objects. Attach a lightweight log or tarp to a long rope and have your horse drag it from Point A to Point B. This simulates moving fallen branches and other objects out of the way on the trail. Start with a VERY long rope. Do NOT wrap the rope around your hand. If the horse panics, drop the rope and begin again, this time with the rider on the ground, dragging the very long rope.

Gate. Practice opening and closing gates while mounted.

Back up on a trail. Mark the course with chalk, paint, or scuffs in the dirt. Go forward, then back up. For a greater challenge, back up around a corner.

Step or walk over cavallettis, boards, logs or branches, to simulate navigating through trail debris.

Trot over poles (cavalletti). Use tree branches or landscape timbers placed 3-4 feet apart. Move the poles around—a real trail does not provide obstacles placed at an ideal trotting width. Put two poles close together and ask your horse to step over both with a single stride; spread them apart and ask him to take a stride between them, and so forth.

Practice putting on and taking off a raincoat while mounted. With timid horses, start this exercise with the rider on the ground, then progress to doing it while mounted.

Walk over tarps. This simulates crossing water for those who live in hydraulically challenged environments and is also a good trust exercise.

You can use your imagination to simulate both normal trail conditions and unusual situations. And be sure to keep a sugar packet in your pockets, just in case you meet a helicopter on the trail someday!

Good riding partners still like to hang out together after a long day on the trail. Susan Kellogg and Kathy Thompson wait for their horses to be judged for the Best Condition award at Renegade Rendezvous 2012.

CHAPTER 4
GETTING HELP ALONG THE WAY

More than many other equestrian sports, training in endurance is easier—and more fun—when it's done with a little help from your friends.

But what if you don't have any friends yet who are endurance riders? This chapter provides suggestion on how to reach out to professionals and to new friends who can help you with your endurance goals. I will also offer you a few ideas *(bad* ideas, obviously) about training partners, as presented by the Bad Idea Fairy.

Vet, farrier, and more

Most seasoned endurance riders agree that developing a professional horse-health support team is a valuable investment of time. There may be several respectable vet hospitals nearby or, conversely, equine vets may be scarce on the ground locally. Finding them may require some legwork on your part.

Talk to other horse owners about veterinary services. Don't just ask if they have a good vet; ask additional questions, like the following:

- Does your vet specialize in equine care?
- Does the vet respond quickly and appropriately in emergency situations?
- Does your vet recommend appropriate routine care for your horse, or do you sometimes feel the vet is looking for more ways to take your money?
- Does the vet handle your horse safely during exams?
- Is it relatively easy to get an appointment for routine care, or is the wait absurdly long?
- Is it easy to communicate with your vet via phone or email?
- Does the vet arrive on time for farm calls or notify you promptly when there is a delay?
- Is the technology used by your vet's office up-to-date and in good repair, or is the X-ray machine out of commission whenever you inquire?
- Other points to investigate when looking for a veterinarian include the following:

- Is the vet certified (or working towards certification) by the American Board of Veterinary Practitioners? Many excellent veterinarians are not, but a board-certified vet is one who has demonstrated expertise in a broad range of clinical subjects and who can communicate medical observations and data in an organized, professional manner.
- Does the vet seem interested in attending classes, reading papers, or doing further research in the skills needed by endurance veterinarians?
- Has the vet ever attended an endurance ride?

Because appropriate foot care is vital for a long-distance horse, finding a competent farrier is also critical. A horse may be able to squeak through years of casual riding with hooves that are poorly shod or infrequently trimmed, but endurance requires rigorous hoof maintenance. Ask other riders—specifically endurance riders—in your area for recommendations. A farrier who works mainly on stack-shod Tennessee Walkers, for example, will not have the expertise in trimming a horse whose job is to "get down the trail efficiently." Find a farrier who is not only experienced doing the work you need done, but also onewho isn't trying to shoe 6 or more horses in a day. Working under a horse is tiring, and the quality diminishes after the 4th shoeing of the day. If your horse is being trimmed but not shod, it's okay to be the 6th or 8th horse in line, as long as all the other horses are also just being trimmed.

Provide a safe, level, well-lit area for your farrier to work.

Do your farrier and your vet a favor and work with your horse *beforehand* so that he is comfortable standing still while being trimmed, shod, or poked full of holes with vaccination needles. Most horses will do this only if they have practiced the skills necessary to stand quietly under such circumstances.

Treat your health-care team with respect and care, and be there *every time* they work on your horse. Ask questions and take notes; a professional will be pleased to talk with you. Provide a safe location for your vet or farrier to work, with a solid, level surface where they and your horse can stand comfortably. Good lighting is important—if natural light is not sufficient, find some other way to light the space. Clean your horse up before the vet or farrier arrives—nobody wants to trim a muddy foot, or inject vaccines into a hide that's caked with dirt. And while it is not necessary to provide a full banquet, why not offer a cup of coffee in winter or some iced tea in summer?

And most importantly, if you're going to bounce any check, do not let it be the check to your vet or farrier!

Consider recruiting other professional practitioners for your health-care team. An equine dentist will keep your horse not only eating efficiently, but comfortable in his bridle. An equine chiropractor or massage therapist can ease minor discomforts before they become more painful injuries.

The Internet provides opportunities to meet and learn from knowledgeable people all over the world. In addition to the Ridecamp listserv hosted by www.endurance.net there are coaches, trainers, and bloggers who offer general and specific advice to address whatever your training issues are. Many riders begin their search for other riders—and vets, trainers, mentors—online, where they often find wonderful information and a large and helpful distance-riding community.

Be aware, of course, that anyone can say anything online… and somewhere out there you will come across the worst possible advice on any subject. The Bad Idea Fairy has a large and talented family, and you will find her cousins online, offering advice that usually turns out to be disastrous!

Read blogs, listservs, and discussion groups (there is a useful list of these in Appendix A) with your intuition in high gear and your common sense on high alert. Triangulate information; check out claims. Trust, but verify. Ask for guidance, but do your research and think for yourself.

Finding a good endurance mentor

You have already discovered one mentor to assist you in surviving and thriving in your first few years of endurance competition: this book! As my own mentor told me (when handing me an article to read), "Paper wisdom will hold still for anybody."

A good mentor will improve the view - and point out the holes.

Still, many people would love to also have personalized advice and guidance from a live person. But where do you find such a person?

Start by reading *Endurance News* and the regional endurance newsletter; ask your vet and farrier; volunteer at a ride or two and talk to other riders. Join your regional endurance or distance-riding group if one exists, and introduce yourself to people wherever you go.

Most importantly, trust your instinct. Certain people call themselves an authority, but if their practices differ significantly from other successful riders, proceed with caution. Be leery of a person who talks a lot but doesn't ride much, or of someone who insists that a mentee "drink the Kool-Aid" and follow instructions blindly.

You can check the ride history of any person who has participated in AERC-sanctioned rides between 1985 and the present (there is usually a delay of 1-2 months for new data). If a person *claims* to have buckets of successful endurance completions, you will be able to find the records on the AERC website (www.aerc.org; look under "AERC Records" and "Rider History"). If the person has many completions but also seems to have ridden a lot of different horses, click the links to the horse history: do most of those horses continue to compete with other riders, or do they just "disappear"?

Talk to experienced riders about *their* mentors—you will probably hear a few names repeated often. Seek out anyone that successful riders consider an authority, ask for help, and don't be surprised when someone agrees to mentor you, either formally or informally. Endurance riders are often very generous when it comes to helping other riders.

Do some "passive learning" by watching equestrians you admire either in person or on video. See how they handle situations; if their actions seem workable for you, copy them. However, know that an experienced rider may only appear to take shortcuts when communicating with a horse. If the horse/rider team has worked together for years, you will not necessarily see the horse learning a skill; you may only see the horse executing the skill. Don't expect your horse to know everything that the experienced horse knows until you teach him.

Ask other riders–someone may be happy to give or loan back issues.

Finding a good instructor

There's a story about the student who wished to learn karate.

He approached a karate master and asked to be accepted as a student.

"It's not me you want as an instructor," demurred the master. "Let me take you to my teacher."

Like the karate student, a rider who wishes to excel in the sport of endurance will want to seek out an instructor who will teach mastery of riding for long distance. Many distance riders cross-train their horses in another discipline, such as dressage or western pleasure, in order to improve the horse and rider communication and to maximize their efficiency on the trail. However, some instructors are most experienced in preparing students to compete in shows, which may not be the best focus for an endurance rider.

When seeking an instructor, look for one who is experienced in teaching what you want to learn, preferably to people in your age group and at your skill level.

You also want to find an atmosphere that suits your learning style. Do you like to be pushed out of your comfort zone or praised extravagantly? Do you prefer boisterous enthusiasm or quiet correction? Are you motivated by a "drill sergeant" approach, or does hollering frighten you? Do you want your instructor to *show* you what you need to learn, or to *describe the process* to you, or to *position your body correctly* so that you can practice correctly? These preferences are individual and unique, and some instructors will suit you better than others.

When seeking an instructor, always look carefully at a facility, their programs, and the manner in which the horses are treated. Use the same sort of criteria you would use to find a day care center for your child. Is it safe, clean, and relatively quiet? Or is it dangerous, dirty, or poorly run? Are the horses sleek or ribby? Are their feet neatly trimmed or shaggy? Is the tack clean and in good repair, or held together with baling string?

You should also watch lessons in progress, or take a lesson or two before committing to an instructor. Make sure you are comfortable with the premises, the instructor's style, and the lesson goals. Listen to what the instructor and students say about the program, and compare what they say to what you see: do the words match the vision?

If not, keep looking.

In the meantime, keep an eye out for events where you might make connections and learn useful skills as well. Trail trial competitions are gaining in popularity nationwide, and although the distance covered is tiny by endurance standards, the opportunity for "positive novelty training" is worth your time. Moving cattle, working with a drill team, or participating in local game days can all be fun and provide excellent training in communication for you and your horse.

Finding a good riding partner

If you ride long distances, you'll discover that some people make the miles pass quickly… others make them seem endless. The distance seems infinite. You'd think that it would be easy to define what kind of people make good riding partners. But, remember that, as with so many things, individual preferences will determine the sort of person (or people) you enjoy spending your trail time with. Riding partners are not required, either—many people prefer to ride alone. Still, for those who are new to the sport, it's fun to meet up with distance riders in your area and ride some miles together. Time will tell if you are well-suited as riding partners.

Here are some things to consider when choosing a partner.

A good riding partner is happy to see you. Even in the rain, even when it's been a crummy day, even when YOU have had a crummy day. A good riding partner knows that a good ride will make everything better.

A good riding partner knows when to take a break. Ripe blackberries by the side of a trail are a good reason for me to stop for a snack. Beautiful scenery is a reason to stop and take a photo. So are Elvis sightings, which occur when a rider shouts, "I see Elvis—look, over there!" and the rest of the group politely looks off into the distance while the shouter hops off into the bushes to pee. (A good riding partner has approximately the same time/distance between pee stops as you. That way, one person isn't always waiting for the other).

A good riding partner knows the viewpoints because they have a camera too!

A good riding partner gets along with your friends and makes them feel welcome.

A good riding partner will support you while you work on your horse's training issues and will ask for your support as well. For example, in one riding group there might be an experienced horse who sets a reasonable pace, a greener horse who needs to practice keeping a steady rhythmic trot, a cranky horse who needs practice working with a group, and a dingbat horse who needs practice focusing on the trail instead of on the invisible monsters that exist only in his mind. A good partner will accommodate them all.

A good riding partner rides safely and helps you to ride safely. She (or he) won't laugh when you carefully describe your planned route and estimated return time to a third party so that, if things go wrong, someone will know where to send help. A good riding partner will help you learn to navigate trails safely and won't rush your learning process.

A good riding partner's horse will go down the trail well with your horse. Not all horses are compatible on the trail: besides the issue of personality, there is the issue of speed in each gait. For example, I rarely ride an event with my friend Paul, although we love to ride together. My big Standardbred mare travels fastest at the trot on flat terrain and up hills, whereas Paul's little Paso Fino gelding travels fastest at a brisk corto down hills. Our overall speed on a 50-mile course averages out, but we find ourselves "leapfrogging." On one 100-mile ride in 2007, we leapfrogged all day, and then stuck together (at a much slower speed) after dark. Individually, we could have finished the course significantly faster if we had continued to leapfrog through the night, but decided that companionship for ourselves and our horses in the dark was more important that a shorter completion time.

If you train for long-distance riding with a partner or a group, you may end up spending as much time with them as you do with your family during the ride season. Do yourself a favor: choose partners that make the miles enjoyable and the trails seem shorter.

The Bad Idea Fairy
might be your training partner if...

Your horse is covered with bite and/or kick marks after a training ride.

You had two flat tires and got lost when she insisted on taking a short-cut to the trailhead.

She brought a can of beans for lunch on the trail... and insisted that you eat some too.

She canters up every hill, regardless of the fitness level of her horse (or yours).

You realize that she finishes top ten in every ride because her horse won't whoa.

She tailgates your "red-ribboned" mare to "teach that horse how to behave."

She won't wear a helmet because it would mess up her outfit.

don't follow the Bad Idea Fairy

ACF Phenomenon, ridden by Susan Powell, and Midnight Sky's Shiraz, ridden by Mona Thacker, are experienced campaigners who see a puddle as a watering hole, not an obstacle.

CHAPTER 5
HITTING THE TRAIL

From purple mountains' majesty to a road through the middle of town, endurance rides can be—and are—held on any type of terrain that will support horse traffic. There is an endurance ride to suit all kinds of riders.

If you live and train near a ridecamp, you and your horse will be familiar with the type of terrain and obstacles you may encounter on ride day. Often, however, you may live an hour, or many hours, distant, and the area may be completely new to you and your horse. That's one of the attractions of endurance riding: events allow you to see some of the world's most beautiful trails from the back of a horse.

This chapter discusses some of the land features and obstacles that you will encounter in training and on an endurance ride, along with tips on teaching and travelling them safely. IN ALL CASES, take new obstacles slowly and carefully, allowing your horse time to consider each situation and to develop trust in your judgment. Building trust will be the most important thing you accomplish when facing obstacles together.

Hills

A rule-of-thumb for hills: travel uphill at a speed that will allow the horse to trot without distress once he reaches the top of the hill.

For a young, green, or unfit horse, or for one returning to work after a long layoff, I dismount and walk hills on foot beside the horse. For steep hills or with an unfit horse, I ride the entire hill at a walk. With a more fit horse, we trot part way and walk the remainder, or trot one-third, walk one-third, and trot again on the last third. If the horse is huffing and puffing at the peak of the hill, we've gone too quickly. A very fit horse can easily canter up a moderately steep hill and then trot on when the grade levels out or drops down.

This is where a heart rate monitor or stethoscope can provide useful information on the fitness of a horse. With a less fit horse, try to keep his heart rate under 160-180 beats per minute when travelling up hills. When you reach the top, note how quickly his heart rate drops below 140-120 beats per minute. As his fitness increases, his recovery time will improve, but before you go racing up the trail, read about evaluating equine fitness in Chapter 7.

Even the little hills will look huge to your horse at first.

Downhill speeds depend somewhat on a horse's experience and skills. An endurance veterinarian told me years ago that a horse has a limited number of "downhill" miles—and that the rider won't know what that number is until they've gotten too close to it. Gaited horses typically utilize their special four-beat easy gait to travel briskly downhill, avoiding the pounding concussion that occurs in a downhill two-beat trot. A well-balanced trotting horse can move downhill at speed, but he should first be taught to carry his weight strongly on his hindquarters in order to avoid excessive concussion on his forehand that can cause front-end lameness. Dressage practice will teach your horse to collect and carry his weight on the hindquarters, and will teach you to help him balance while he does this.

When in doubt, slow down a little. If you've ever seen the movie "Man from Snowy River," you will remember Jim Craig plunging off a steep cliff on his horse, leaving the other horses and riders at the top. This is a terrific stunt to watch, but a dumb one to try. Preserve the longevity of your distance horse by taking descents carefully.

Creeks and puddles

Horse eyes don't have the same kind of depth perception that human eyes have, which explains why the rider sees a perfectly normal mud puddle and the horse apparently sees a bottomless pit swarming with crocodiles. Depending on the light and reflection, horses literally can't tell if that water has a bottom or not and, being prey animals, they opt to avoid falling into the water and through the center of the earth.

With experience and practice, horses learn that if it *smells* like a puddle, and it's *shaped* like a puddle, and there was a puddle in the same location last week, and there are hoof prints leading *out* of the puddle on the other side, then it's probably okay to wade on through it.

When teaching a horse to cross water, choose a puddle or stream that cannot be avoided by jumping or stepping off-trail. Face your horse to a great big splashy bit—wide, but not necessarily deep. Do not holler, do not scream. Your voice and body should be quiet.

Try to communicate—calmly—the following thoughts to your horse:

We are not leaving until we've crossed this water. HINT: Do not begin this training an hour before sunset. Start before noon, just in case… and maybe pack a lunch (and a book).

We are not going anywhere but through this water. "Back to the trailer" is not an option unless we first cross the water and then cross it again in the other direction.

We do not need to look good crossing this water. We do not get extra points for crossing in a dignified manner the first time.

There is no shame in asking for help from another person or another horse. Many horses will trust the leadership of a calm horse and will follow promptly, if nervously.

We do not need to go through this water head first. Tail first is a time-honored way to cross water the first time. Our goal is to keep the hair side facing up. Beyond that, anything goes. It's okay for the rider to walk beside the horse through a puddle. However, do NOT do this if your horse is likely to freak out and leap, because chances are you're the thing he'll leap onto.

Practice crossing where the footing is solid and the water is too wide to leap over.

It's okay to pause mid-puddle or mid-stream, especially if your horse is inclined to leap or rush. At first, pause for a breath or two. Gradually build up to stopping for a count of 30… 60… 120… and so on, until your horse can stand quietly in the water.

Your goal is for your horse to approach, cross, and exit water calmly and routinely. Keep that goal in mind and ask for help from a friend or trainer if the horse is adamantly opposed to or sincerely afraid of crossing water. And obviously, you want to do this only with puddles you know are *safe*—if you suspect that there may be broken glass, trash, or worse at the bottom of the water, go around it!

Sometimes, having a trusted horse lead the way is all that is required to convince a steed to proceed. Sometimes, you may need all of your wits *and* a long rope to get him across. Take your time, be patient, don't give up. Water crossing is an important skill.

Sand and mud

Sand and mud have something very important in common: they are tendon-strainers, especially for horses who do not regularly train in deep sand or on slick mud. Yet, with slow practice, horses can strengthen their tendons as they gain skill and learn to balance while navigating through sand and mud. Be prepared to spend months practicing in deep sand and mud before asking for speed or distance—that way, the time you spend building a base will not be interrupted by mandatory stall rest, which is what your vet will prescribe if your horse injures a tendon.

Sand. Moving around in deep sand is exhausting. It is like wearing ankle weights, and for a horse unaccustomed to the extra drag on their feet and lower legs, it is easy to strain a suspensory tendon, an injury that can take a long time to heal. And yet, horses at those beach-front tourist rides carry squealing out-of-towners across dunes of soft, deep sand all day long. How do they do it?

The best way to strengthen any set of muscles or tendons is to do it *gradually.* Do not start out expecting to trot briskly through five miles of deep sand. *Walk* through a mile of it. Then, stop and rest. If you're skeptical about the difficulty, hop off and slog beside your horse for a mile; it's likely that *you* won't mind a break after 15 minutes. Add distance or speed—not both at the same time—in increments.

Mud. The "dragging down" sensation of grippy mud is similar to the heavy feeling of deep sand, with an added strain of slipping, sliding, and the sensation of each foot being sucked off the end of the leg. As with sand, it is possible to teach a horse to navigate relatively gracefully through mud, but practicing this skill should be done gradually, with good balance between horse and rider. In deep mud, a barefooted horse has an advantage over a horse wearing hoof boots or horse shoes: his footwear won't get left behind in the muck. He may also have slightly better traction on a slippery mud surface; however, skill in maneuvering through mud can be learned by any horse.

5.1: Different types of mud

There are different *types* of mud: I attended an endurance ride once that had beautiful arena-like dirt footing on the day before the ride, but when the rain started falling at 7 a.m. on ride day, the trails quickly turned to mud. My mare, who lives and trains in a maritime climate, soon figured out that the reddish mud (clay) was slippery and the blackish mud (gravel) was gritty, and after a few miles she was rating her own speed depending on the type of mud she faced. We took extra-long to finish, but we were able to complete a 50-mile ride with my horse showing no signs of undue fatigue or soreness.

Ice, snow, rocks, and other hazardous surface factors

Ice: As with mud, ice has the potential to be slippery. It also has the potential to be crunchy. Crunchy ice is not a problem for traction, once the horse has learned to punch his hooves through the surface to the (hopefully) more solid ground below. Be aware that crunchy ice can cut and abrade the skin of your horse's lower legs, so try to keep your experience with crunchy ice at a minimum once you've learned how to negotiate through it together.

Slick ice, by contrast, can be very hazardous. Depending on the extent of the iciness, you may be able to find firmer ground and better footing by going slightly off of the established trail and into the bushes. If the ice is extensive and very slick, stay home. Some hazards are best avoided.

Snow: Snow, like ice, can be crunchy or slick. If the snow is slippery and you do not feel safe walking through the snow on your own feet, don't go there on horseback.

Otherwise, allow your horse to pick a path and help him to stay balanced as he moves by keeping your weight quiet in the saddle. Working in very deep, heavy, or wet snow is hard work, and a horse in a heavy winter coat can overheat. Be considerate and don't push him too hard, especially while he is learning.

Rocks: Rocks on the trail are a common cause of lameness in competition. A large rock can cause a stone bruise, smaller rocks can irritate sole of a tender-footed horse, and sand can abrade the lower leg inside hoof boots and gaiters. Teach your horse to watch his feet by walking slowly through rocky portions of the trail. Allow him the time to figure out how to go around bigger rocks. If he is tender footed even after extensive conditioning, hoof boots or pads added to steel shoes can protect the soles from cuts and bruising by rocks. Rinse sand from your horse's legs whenever possible if he is prone to abrasions.

Pavement: The surface itself can be hazardous. Pavement offers two major challenges: concussion and lack of grip.

The concussion of pavement, if approached with the same type of gradual loading over time that you would practice with deep sand, can actually build bone. Standardbreds on the racetrack are started slowly on hard surface work at a young age; by the time they are old enough to race, their legs and feet have grown strong and sturdy. If the roads that you ride on are relatively flat, begin with walking and gradually add short stretches of trotting—25 strides at a time.

Pavement on hills offer a different problem for horses: slipping. A steel-shod horse will need to learn to manage his feet, or risk careening clumsily to a crash on the road. Barefoot horses seem to do better, and hoof boots offer a measure of grip. My own steel-shod horses navigate stretches of hilly paved road every week without difficulty, but I am careful not to rush them or unbalance them as they travel.

Roads offer the additional challenge of mailboxes (which, for some reason, scare the ears off of many horses) and white painted lines (which are perceived by many horses as gaping chasms to be leapt over… onto the slippery pavement).

Roadside monsters: Not all roadside monsters are imaginary. Riding on the road puts you close to traffic (which may or may not slow down), barking dogs, and roadside garbage. Be careful, and don't be afraid to dismount for safety.

Monsters!

Logs and branches

Fallen logs: In many regions, it's impossible for ride managers to completely clear 50 miles or more of trail, and so small "hop-over" logs are sometimes left in place. Your goal is to cross them without breaking stride. If you are walking, your horse walks over the log and continues walking on the other side. If you are trotting, he trots without leaping; if you are cantering, he stretches his stride up and over without changing his rhythm.

If the hop-over is large, feel free to slow down in order to cross it, or to look for an alternate route. You may wish to teach your horse a verbal cue to signal stepping over an obstacle so that you are both ready to cross at the same time.

Branches: If thick tree branches or other "brushy" obstacles block the trail, teach your horse to navigate through them calmly, quietly, and thoughtfully. Take your time: getting tangled in branches is scary for a horse when he is rushed through the process. Hobble training helps accustom your horse to the feeling of stuff around his feet and lower legs, so that he learns to move without panicking.

Whoops, aka whoop-de-doos

There is probably a proper technical term for these trail features, but the dirt bikers who create them call them "whoops." Whoops are big dips and bumps carved into the trail tread by dirt bikes. Peak to peak they are 4 to 8 feet across and a source of great joy to bikers. For horses, however, whoops are a nightmare. They are just far enough apart that a horse would prefer to trot them. However, once the peak is reached it is easy to misstep and strain a tendon.

As a rider, your best bet is to walk through sections of whoops, or to trot them in a very collected frame with deliberate care given to each stride. If you'd like to avoid whoops without making enemies of other trail users, consider clearing a flat path alongside them that horses can use.

Narrow trail

You only need to mash your knees on a tree trunk once or twice to recognize the need to steer your horse deliberately on narrow trails. Your horse will naturally try to avoid going between trees when he knows his belly won't fit, but he might not remember that your legs hang at his sides, right in the "bonk zone."

Here's how to help him: as you travel down a narrow trail and spot a potentially knee-banging tree ahead, point your horse's *head* at the tree. This is counterintuitive: if you want the horse to avoid the tree, you'd think you would aim him away from it. However, if the trail is narrow, he doesn't have a lot of choice about where his feet go—but you can influence where his *barrel* is by moving his head: if his head is pointed at the tree, his barrel will move away from it, and your knee is saved!

This technique is also effective on narrow cliff trails. Again, bend your horse's head and neck towards the outside (drop-off) edge of the cliff in order to bend his barrel to the inside (high side) of the trail.

Bridges

Trip-trap. Trip-trap. Trip-trap.

Horses know darn well that there is a *troll* under every bridge. Horses are also convinced that the size of the troll is inversely proportionate to the size of the bridge span. Big bridges have little trolls. Little bridges have big trolls. Why take a chance? According to your horse, the trails are *just as nice on this side of the river.*

But someday you will NEED to cross the bridge. Better to learn to cross it when you want to, rather than wait until it's an emergency.

This green horse is "sandwiched" between two experienced horses when they cross the bridge.

Crossing a bridge is a lot like crossing water, without the "tail first" option. Please do not try to walk a reluctant horse backwards over a bridge.

Everything else still applies. Once again, try to communicate the following to your horse:

We are not leaving until we've crossed this ~~water~~ bridge.

We are not going in any direction other than ~~through this water~~ over this bridge. "Back to the trailer" isn't an option unless we first cross the ~~water~~ bridge and then cross again the other direction.

We do not need to look good crossing this ~~water~~ bridge. We do not get extra points for crossing in a dignified manner the first time.

There is no shame in asking for help from another person or another horse.

It's okay to pause mid-~~puddle~~ bridge, especially if your horse is inclined to leap or rush.

You know your horse best, so think ahead about what you can do to make bridge-crossing routine and easy for him. And who knows? He might even cross it promptly and without fuss the very first time you point him at it. But if he doesn't, have a plan ready. Here are some suggestions:

Send a trusted "buddy" horse over the bridge first. If it's a long bridge, ask the buddy horse to stop part way across and wait for you. If the buddy gets too far away, your horse may panic at the separation and do something dumb.

Dismount and walk beside your horse across the bridge. Do not choose this option if you suspect your horse will freak and leap, because he might leap on top of you.

Bracket your horse with *two* trustworthy horse friends. One horse leads—the rider might even have a lead rope attached to your horse. You ride, with encouraging voice and legs. The final horse follows, "pushing" your reluctant mount ahead. It doesn't have to be pretty, but it does need to be safe.

When he does reach the far side, always reward your horse with verbal praise or a cookie.

Depending on his degree of acceptance, decide whether or not to repeat the exercise immediately. If he crossed the bridge relatively effortlessly and was delighted by the cookie on the far side, do it again and give him another cookie (then do it once more so you can continue your ride). If he put up a huge struggle and is mentally tired, walk away from the bridge and let him think about the experience. Either way, crossing the bridge should be easier the second time you do it.

Hikers, dogs, and other horses

Hikers on the trail can be a terrifying surprise to a horse. Sometimes the hikers are carrying backpacks, fishing poles, or other equipment that make them look entirely unlike a human who might be carrying cookies.

Help your horse understand that hikers are *people* by calling a cheery "good morning" when you spot them ahead on the trail. Try to get them to say something if they don't answer your greeting, either by asking a question about the trail ahead (even if you know the answer) or by telling them, "My horse doesn't know that you are a human—could you say 'hi' to him and maybe feed him this cookie?" I carry horse treats in my pockets for times like these.

Dogs on the trails often don't have experience around horses. Even a well-trained dog is sometimes tempted to chase or nip at a fast-moving horse. Slow down or stop to minimize the temptation. If the dog is on-leash, but leaping and barking wildly as you approach, stop at a distance and allow the owner to calm the dog or move it off the trail so you can pass. Speak to the dog in a happy, friendly, good-dog voice so that it will know that *you* are a human and not just part of a gigantic two-headed prey animal. Be polite, but stay safe: if the dog seems aggressive or there are several uncontrolled dogs off-leash, be prepared to change your direction or detour around them.

Assume every animal you encounter is "in training."

Moving around other horses on the trail offers a unique challenge. At an endurance ride, you can expect to pass and be passed by other horses on the trail. If your horse objects to this, you need to work with him so that he can behave safely in a group of other horses, unruly or otherwise.

Mastery of this skill will include the following:

Your horse is trotting down the trail (alone or in a group) and sees other horses ahead. His ears may go up, his nostrils may flare, but his gait and pace remain unchanged, and he does *not* pull your arms out of their sockets.

Your horse is trotting down the trail (alone or in a group) and sees other horses ahead. Without speeding up, you overtake the horses, and then ask for permission to pass. The horses ahead slow down, move aside, and you and your horse go on by with no tail swishing, no ear pinning, and no equine drama of any kind.

Your horse is trotting down the trail (alone or in a group) and a horse trots up behind you. The rider greets you in a friendly way, and then asks you to "yield the trail" (this is not always formal). You and your horse slow down a bit, move aside, and the other horse and rider go on by with no equine drama.

For some horses, this is easy. For others, it is a struggle. Know your horse—if he needs practice, start practicing.

If your horse is body shy, gather a group of riding buddies and load their pockets with cookies. When your horse gets close to a friend, the friend can offer a cookie or a scratch on the face. Do this while standing still at first, then gradually work up to doing it while moving. Keep safety in mind and pay attention to the body language of the entire group of horses while doing this exercise.

Stump Bears, Log Gators, and Rock Panthers

As noted in the section about crossing water, horses don't see the world the same way humans see it. Their depth perception is different due to the mechanics and placement of their eyes and, more importantly, their priorities are different because horses evolved as prey animals, not as predators. Their first reaction to any new object or smell or situation will always be filtered through an instinctive drive to *leave the lions far behind.*

Not all horses are easily spooked. Not all horses remain easy to spook. How did those horses learn to settle down? That's the million dollar question. Here are a few tips for managing the horse that is still learning:

A thinking horse is not as prone to idiocy. If you are able to focus your horse's brain on other things in some way as he works, he will be less inclined to see scary monsters lurking along the trail. Ask for bending, flexing, shoulder-in, collection, or whatever physical task it takes to direct his thoughts out through the bit and up the reins, rather than up through the feet and out the ears.

A horse who knows what will *probably* happen doesn't worry so much and seek escape from fear by spooking. Worry-prone horses are reassured by routine.

Sometimes, real life doesn't follow the routine. A tire goes flat, your riding partner gets the flu and stays home, or the weather falls apart. If your horse is a Type A worrier who frets about change in routine, get him accustomed to frequent changes until he understands that changes in routine are, well, *routine.*

An experienced horse that has seen lots of weird stuff that didn't kill him won't worry as much if he sees something new and weird. *(Remember the helicopter incident in Chapter 3?)*

Which of these would scare your horse?

If you see something on the trail ahead that you suspect will push your horse's "idiot button", eyeball the obstacle and then *look away from it.* If you focus your own attention by staring at something, you will also stiffen your own body—which is your horse's cue that you have perceived a threat. By allowing your own eyes to sweep past the potential terror, you communicate clearly to your horse that you see the object and are not worried about it.

5.2: Harmless or Monstrous? Only your horse knows for sure.

On the road near my house, trash cans are set out for pickup on the weekday that I normally ride, and my horse feels obligated to give these the evil eye even if the can is in EXACTLY the same place it had been the week before. If you consider her perspective, however, you understand that the suspicion is well-placed. The trash can *looks* the same as last week, but it might *smell* completely different, depending on what was thrown away that week. My horse believes—and many horses agree with her—that this sort of change is not trustworthy. Be aware of these perceived hazards and be ready to teach your horse how to behave appropriately when encountering them.

Work your way past obstacles safely and without excessive drama. If the horse is concerned but scoots by an object that a few months ago would have had him screaming like a girl, praise him and move along.

Positive experiences with unexpected stuff can lead to acceptance and trust. Practice this—you will need it later.

An endurance horse may use a wide variety of gaits during a competition day. Start out slowly, even though someday you may be in a flying finish at an international event.

CHAPTER 6

HOW LONG? HOW FAR? HOW FAST?

One of the most commonly dispensed pieces of advice about training and conditioning a distance horse is to start with Long Slow Distance, or LSD (not to be confused OR combined with lysergic acid diethylamide).

The problem arises when we start to define our terms: how long is "long" and how slow is "slow"?

The answer, as with so many things about endurance riding, is "it depends."

Totally unhelpful advice? Not really!

This chapter will help you determine how long and how slow to go while training and conditioning your horse. It starts by showing you how to evaluate your horse's current level of fitness, and then gives you examples of how to improve that level of fitness so that you can safely begin to work further and faster. And although technology is wonderful and fun, it is not necessary to buy the latest electronic heart-rate monitor and most expensive GPS to assist you in your training; this chapter provides tips for low-tech and no-tech training.

If your horse has just finished a successful season of three-day eventing or has recently returned from a strenuous week of packing in the wilderness, his fitness level will be higher than the mare who has recently weaned a foal. The fitness programs for these horses will be very different.

How long is long?

Write down everything you can remember about the activities your horse has been involved in over the past year. If he's been attending horse shows, trail rides, jumping lessons, cow clinics, or similar activities, he will have a base layer of fitness even if those experiences don't apply directly to endurance rides. A horse who has recently been pregnant, recovered from illness or injury, or who just hasn't been out of the pasture much will need to be started more slowly. Once he becomes fit, this horse will probably be able to perform in distance work just as well as a horse who has not been laid up.

An experienced trail horse will already have many skills needed for long-distance work.

Jabba the Hutt

Let's start with Jabba the Hutt, an overweight pasture ornament who is healthy and sound, but hasn't done much more than eat for at least a year. If your horse is more fit than Jabba, skip down to the section about **The Cheerleader.**

This "Jabba" needed a lot of long, slow work to get fit.

Jabba needs to start slowly, with 15 to 20 minutes of work at a walk a few times during the first week. From there add 5 to 10 minutes of work to each session each week. By the end of a month, Jabba will be able to work from 35 minutes to 1 hour without fainting. When you have achieved workouts of an hour (walking), you will be ready to add some trot work, although without adding time yet.

When building up a horse's fitness level, add *speed* or *time*, but not simultaneously.

After Jabba can work comfortably at a walk for an hour, substitute 10 minutes of trotting for 10 minutes of walking as part of the hour-long workout. The next week, add 10 minutes of walking to the total workout, so he is moving for 1 hour and 10 minutes—1 hour of walking plus 10 minutes of trotting. The next week, up his trot time to 20 minutes, so that he is trotting for 20 minutes and walking for 50 minutes. Note that the trot sessions do not need to be 10 continuous minutes. A sample session for Jabba after he's been working for 6 weeks:

Walk	20 minutes
Trot	3 minutes
Walk	10 minutes

Trot	5 minutes
Walk	10 minutes
Trot	2 minutes
Walk	20 minutes

When Jabba is fit enough for sessions longer than an hour, try to take a riding lesson or two with him each month. A good trainer will be able to spot and help you to correct weaknesses in Jabba's form or in yours. Gradually replace Jabba's walking workout with trot work until you are only walking for a warm-up and cool-down, and as trail terrain demands.

When Jabba the Hutt can trot for 20 to 30 minutes without needing to be carried home in your arms, he can switch to the Cheerleader's training schedule.

The Cheerleader

The Cheerleader is the horse who, although she hasn't been ridden much in the past year, is not sluggish or overweight. The Cheerleader is the one who runs around her pasture several times a day, head up, tail flagged. She does not need the basic fitness routine required by Jabba the Hutt, but she still needs to build muscle and skill in order to carry a rider for long periods of time. If your horse is more fit than the Cheerleader, skip down to the section marked The Weekend Warrior.

This young stallion looks fit, but he is not strong enough to carry a rider over distance yet.

The Cheerleader can start with 20-minute sessions of walking and trotting two or three times a week. Build up her ability to carry the rider by working her over ground poles or low obstacles on the trail.

As with Jabba's routine, her workouts should be lengthened gradually and trot work added to the session after two or three weeks, making sure to add speed or time to a workout, but not both on the same day. Riding lessons twice a month or more will give you another set of "eyes on the ground" to help locate weaknesses that can be strengthened. Here's a sample session for the Cheerleader after she's been working for 6 weeks:

Walk	10 minutes
Trot	5 minutes
Walk	5 minutes
Trot	10 minutes
Walk	10 minutes
Trot	5 minutes
Walk	15 minutes

When the Cheerleader can work for an hour of mostly trotting, she can take up the training schedule of the Weekend Warrior.

The Weekend Warrior

The Weekend Warrior is the horse who has been ridden steadily for the last 6 months (or more). Perhaps he has been used as a lesson horse, or a cow horse, or even a racehorse (my first endurance mare came to me straight from the harness track). The Weekend Warrior is fit, but he doesn't yet have the knowledge, skill, or fitness to carry a rider over uneven terrain at a trot for the long distances of an endurance event.

Sometimes it's not the body but the mind that needs conditioning..

Work the Weekend Warrior on trails as much as possible, teaching him to negotiate different kinds of terrain and trail conditions. Start at a walk if he hasn't done much trail work recently, and add trot work gradually.

An hour of training should not tire him, so add time or speed in 5- to 10-minute increments. As always, don't add time *and* speed in the same workout.

Here is a sample session for the Weekend Warrior after he's been working for 6 weeks:

Walk	10 minutes
Trot	5 minutes
Walk	10 minutes
Trot	15 minutes
Walk	10 minutes
Trot	15 minutes
Walk	10 minutes
Trot	10 minutes
Walk	15 minutes

Be sure to train in all kinds of weather as well, although you should not ride for very long when a hurricane or blizzard blows in. Be sure to also incorporate as many types of terrain as possible (details about terrain training can be found in Chapter 5).

Real Life gets in the way

Many riders experience periodic slowdowns in their training schedule as a result of Real Life.

Real Life includes things like a missing horse shoe, a child's piano recital or dental appointment, a flat tire, a week of late nights at work, and the stomach flu.

These setbacks may seem major, but try not to worry too much. Your horse will not lose fitness after a single skipped session, or even after a skipped week of work. Shorten your first workout when you return to training, and then proceed forward, gradually and slowly.

You may have noticed that the training outlines do not dictate how many miles to travel each week in your training. Stick to training for time, rather than distance at first. When you are riding your horse at a mixture of walk and trot for two hours or more, use a basic GPS (most smart phones have a free app for this) to find out how far you are travelling in your average workout. If you are covering 10 miles or more in 2 hours, your pace is adequate for an endurance ride. If you are covering less than 10 miles in 2 hours, add more trot work or practice trotting a little faster.

When you can do 10 miles in 2 hours twice a week, you're ready to start a 25-mile limited distance ride. You probably won't be *first* across the finish line at that pace, but your horse will be fit to do the distance, and as you know, the motto of the sport is "To Finish is to Win."

Keep in mind that the person who finishes the ride in 11th place gets the same ride prize and number of mileage points as the person who finishes dead last... so take it easy and slowly the first year, in order to build up a horse who will then be able to finish and enjoy his events during the second year and, hopefully, for years to come.

But how slow is slow?

You may have noticed that this training regime might require MONTHS to get a green horse or a horse that is unfit ready for that first distance event.

Yep. That's right.

The time to "leg up" or bring a horse into endurance-fit condition can be up to 2 years, depending on the initial fitness of the horse.

The good news—this *doesn't* mean you can't compete until you've trained at home for 2 years, because competing can be part of conditioning. However, please do not expect to create a long-distance champion who can work for years by racing your green or unfit horse at top speed before having built a good conditioning base first.

It is also important to avoid over-conditioning (more about that in Chapter 7). My preferred training program for 50-mile rides includes two or three rides per week, maximum. One of those rides is, ideally, an arena session or dressage lesson and the others are trail rides of 8-14 miles. When training for longer distances (75- to 100-mile events), do not increase the training miles, only the intensity. Remember that once you begin competing, the competitions themselves will serve as training sessions for longer, harder, or faster competitions.

My preferred regime also doesn't include any cantering or galloping. I don't normally *allow* an endurance horse to canter or gallop on trails until the **second or third year** of competition. We practice cantering in the arena. If we want to speed up the pace on the trail, we trot faster. This teaches the horse to rate, the skill of performing a particular gait slower or faster, as requested by the rider. An easily rated horse is a joy on the trail—he can trot through tricky terrain at a slow pace and then speed up without breaking gait when the trail is wide open and clear.

When you trot on the trail, figure out the speed that you and your horse are most comfortable with, and practice it. That is your "all-day trot," and it's different for every horse and rider team. Your speed at a trot may be faster than you expected, or it might be slower. It doesn't matter. Keep that steady pace and you will be able to travel farther than you ever thought possible.

Remember, your goal in endurance is to *finish* the ride. Your best strategy for finishing rides in your first year of competition is to spend as much time as possible in your all-day trot without stopping until the finish line.

How to judge speed without a GPS

Here is a good trick for rating your horse. After using it in a few practice sessions, you will be able to estimate your horse's speed at the trot without a GPS:

Sing.

That's right—*sing.*

Singing to your horse as he trots down the trail helps establish the rhythm that you want him to hold. It relaxes the horse *and* helps the rider build up good breath control. It also improves your posture, because it's hard to sing out while slouching! Singing is a good way to pass the time as you ride and an excellent way to make sure other trail users (like bicyclists or bears) are aware of your presence so that you don't startle them and they don't startle your horse.

The type of song is not important. I sing children's tunes, Boy Scout campfire songs, and sailors' sea shanties because they are rhythmic and have lots of verses. Don't worry about the quality of your voice—your horse won't mind if you miss the high notes.

6.1: My grandma does PT

Here's a jody call that one of my riding partners loves to holler out. He insists that we all holler out the first line and he finishes the couplet. You can do this!

When my grandma was 91

She did PT just for fun

When my grandma was 92

She did PT better than you

When my grandma was 93

She did PT better than me

If you are self-conscious about singing, try some jody calls, also known as marching cadences. These are the traditional call-and-response songs sung by military personnel while running or marching. (ALERT: some traditional jodies are quite risqué and might not be appropriate for mixed groups).

If you sing while you ride, you will notice that certain songs go best with a particular trot speed.

For example, I've discovered that "When the Saints Go Marching In" works well for a trot of 5-6 mph, while "The Battle of New Orleans" is the perfect tempo for my mare's 7-8 mph trot.

Feel free to experiment and invite your riding partners to join in on the chorus or sing their own songs. Figure out which songs go best with what speed, and then you won't be forever dependent on a GPS to determine your speed.

The sport of endurance is supposed to be *fun*, after all—and nothing is more fun than a song to help you move down the trail!

The Bad Idea Fairy writes a training log

Day 1: *Saddle up at dawn and gallop 2 hours. Break for lunch. Gallop 2 hours back to the truck.*

Day 2: *Go to barn at noon. Horse pins ears. Go out to lunch with BFF, share photos of yesterday's ride.*

Day 3: *Saddle up, gallop 2.5 hours. Break for lunch. During lunch break, horse lies down, won't get up. Spend an hour coaxing horse up, then walk back to truck.*

Day 4: *Shopping day! Go to tack store and buy new outfits.*

Days 5-12: *Busy, can't ride.*

Day 13: *Saddle up. Horse flinches when saddle is lifted. Apply Desitin® and duct tape to the open sores on his back. Then saddle up, gallop 3 hours.*

Three months later... *Horse has complete outfit in matching colors, including braiding bands and little pom poms on the fly mask. Even the bandages and wound cream are dyed to match.*

Five months later... *Horse looks awesome standing out in the field. Leave him there and go shopping.*

Veteran competitor Dennis Summers gives his horse AH Bantiki a break by "tailing" uphill. Listen to and observe experienced riders — and most of all, pay attention to what your horse tells you about his fitness.

CHAPTER 7
EVALUATING EQUINE FITNESS

As I mentioned earlier, training and legging up (conditioning) an endurance horse is like eating an elephant: you won't be able to do it in one quick go. You might buy a "made horse" (one that has already successfully competed in long-distance competitions), but conditioning is an ongoing process.

This chapter provides you with information about the process of legging up and feeding your endurance horse. We will review some of the science behind the best practices and look at hands-on techniques for measuring the fitness of your horse.

Create a ride log for your horse

Keeping a ride log (formal or informal) is an effective way to track what you and your horse have learned together. The process is gradual, and it is easy to get discouraged if you don't have a way to monitor the progress that you and your horse are making towards your long-distance goals.

Some people track all sorts of details about their horses on a weekly basis, including weight, resting heart rate, rectal temperature, feed routine, training regime, and more. If you love accumulating data, this may be something you enjoy. Look for pre-printed ride logs that some online endurance-tack purveyors sell.

You can also record information electronically, including speed, altitude changes, heart rate, and so forth, using a high-quality GPS. Special software enables you to create elaborate full-color glossy graphs with circles and arrows and a paragraph for each explaining what each one is about. Basic GPS systems are available for many smartphones at low or no cost.

Alternately, you can design your own system for recording information. Keep a spiral-bound notebook and a pencil in your saddle bag and jot down notes about the terrain, the speed and mileage, the training issues you worked on during each session, or even the flora and fauna you saw on your ride.

Blogging is a good tool for me, because I can incorporate a verbal description of trail conditions, speed, and training issues (including the training issues of our riding companions), as well as the temperature and weather. I also use a cheap digital camera to document sessions whenever possible.

Compulsive data collectors may appreciate smartphone apps like Runkeeper.

With all these tools available, you can keep track of the data that is most important to you using the tools and technology that are comfortable. Review your entries periodically and marvel at the progress you make on your journey.

Getting fitter: Developing muscles, nerves, and bones

If you use a heart rate monitor or stethoscope, you will notice changes in your horse's level of cardiovascular fitness as early as 3-4 weeks after you begin a training regime. He will be able to travel further at a slightly faster speed, and his heart rate will recover (drop below 60 beats per minute) quicker. This is a result of changes in the collective characteristics of the muscle fibers.

Improvements in muscle strength are caused by both muscular and neural adaptations. As the muscles change size, shape, and strength, the nervous system itself is learning how best to coordinate motions required by the new work (Steelman, 2008).

However, be aware that the horse's muscles (including his heart) are not the only parts of his body that are undergoing change. Research in Thoroughbred race horses shows that changes in activity also remodel *bones* for up to two years. According to David Nunamaker, VMD PhD, a researcher who has spent 20 years working to understand how bones change, "Bone can only develop based on its own experience. Training adapts bone to training" (as cited in West, 2003).

In other words: your horse's muscles, nerves, and bones will suit endurance competitions only if you train over time the way you intend to compete.

However—and this is *really* important to note—rushing the process can lead to catastrophic injury.

Remember the "Miller Time"

Rest periods between training sessions are vitally important. While some of your workout sessions should challenge your horse to perform at a higher level, it is the time *between* those sessions when his body actually undergoes the changes necessary to improve. Full recovery from a workout session can take a few days to a week or longer (Steelman, 2008).

Rest is essential for your horse's body and mind—he will not only recuperate and heal from any minor boo-boos on his days off, he will also *think* about what happened. You will be pleasantly surprised at how much mental progress can occur during non-training days. When legging up a novice horse, a good rule of thumb is to allow a day off for every 10 miles of training. If you are tempted to ride your horse every single day, don't. A better approach is to work him 2-3 days each week, and take *yourself* to the gym on his days off. Your added fitness will be a bonus in arduous competitions.

Pay attention to your horse's emotional well-being as well as his heart rate and recovery time. If he *looks* weary, it is possible that he needs to slow down or skip a few training sessions. Your noble steed isn't a machine; he's a thinking being. Your goal as a rider is to create an emotional bond with the horse that will make both of you happier—and if your horse feels continually overworked, he will not learn to trust your judgment.

Rest is vital to the health and happiness of an endurance horse in training.

Feed requirements and the Henneke scale

Susan Garlinghouse, DVM MSc, endurance vet and endurance rider, spends a lot of her time talking to riders about the physiology and nutritional needs of hard-working endurance horses. Garlinghouse (2012) recommends the following, listed in order of importance:

Forage (good-quality grass pasture or hay)

Beet pulp

Alfalfa in small amounts (think "sauce" and not "spaghetti")

Good-quality concentrate ration, as needed to maintain a good body condition, and which is targeted to supplement nutrients not adequately provided by forage or hay. For example, in the Pacific Northwest, the soil—and thus, the hay—is notoriously low in selenium, and so a selenium supplement is needful.

Garlinghouse also prefers commercial concentrate rations that are beet-pulp based over trying to mix together a lot of different commodities. The cost of commercial performance feeds may be perceived as higher, but the overall nutrient profile tends to be better for the needs of long-distance horses.

7.1 What is beet pulp?

Beet pulp is the fiber material left over after sugar beets have the sugar processed and removed. It is available in most American feed stores as a pelleted or shredded product. Beet pulp is a highly digestible, low-carbohydrate feed, and most horses find it delicious. It's very high in soluble fiber (carbohydrates) in a good way. Beet pulp is also generally fairly low in simple sugars, but this can vary from batch to batch and depends on whether molasses has been added to help the pelleting process. It contains roughly the same caloric content as oats. Molasses can be mostly removed by soaking a batch of beet pulp, discarding the water, and then adding more water to the mash.

Although the pellets or shreds can be fed dry, most endurance riders soak the feed for 20 minutes or more (a ratio of 3/1 water to beet pulp creates a soft, moist mash — more water can be added to make a sloppier feed). Soaked beet pulp provides horses with hydration, calories, and fiber — all good things for hard-working equines (Haydt, 2009).

What may be the funniest beet pulp story ever told was written by Susan Garlinghouse. You can find a link to the article in the **Footnoted Resources**.

How do you know if your horse is getting enough—but not too much—feed to maintain his level of activity?

The Henneke Body Condition Scoring system is a relatively objective measurement of the layer of fat covering certain skeletal landmarks on the body.

Some locations (such as through the hindquarters or around the tailhead) are areas occupied by muscle as well as fat. You can easily learn to feel the difference between the two with your hands. It is important to assess the areas using hands as well as eyes, as skeletal landmarks can be obscured by fur, mud, or insufficient light. Hold your hand flat with fingers together when exploring the landmarks, and be sure to examine both sides of the horse.

Each landmark area in the Henneke scale is scored independently; the numbers are added together and averaged. Endurance horses in good condition generally score between 4 and 5 on the scale. Thin endurance horses may run out of gas during competition; chubby horses will have to work harder to carry their extra bulk a long distance.

Wood (1995) suggests considering the following key landmark areas:

Loin. An extremely thin horse (2-3 on the scale) will have a ridge down the back where the backbone protrudes. No fat is felt along the back of a thin horse. However, this is one of the first areas to fill in as a horse gains weight. Initially, fat is laid down around the organs and then along the base of the spine. As the horse gets fatter (7-8), an obvious crease or depression forms down the back because of fat accumulation along the spine.

Horses fed in a herd will need extra attention to make sure they are getting the nutrition they need.

Ribs. First, visually assess the rib area, then run your fingers across the rib cage. A very thin horse (2-3) will have prominent ribs, easily seen and felt, with no fat padding. As the horse begins to gain weight, a little padding can be felt around the ribs; by level 5 the ribs will no longer be visible, but can easily be palpated by passing a hand down the rib cage. As the horse progresses towards obesity (7-8), feeling the ribs becomes impossible.

Tailhead. On a very thin horse (up to a 3), the tailhead is prominent and easily discernible. Once the horse starts gaining weight, fat fills in around it. Fat can easily be palpated, and as the horse becomes obese, the fat will feel soft and begin to bulge.

Withers. If a horse is very thin, the underlying structure of the withers will be easily visible. At a level 5, the withers will appear rounded. At levels 6 through 8, varying degrees of fat deposits can be felt along the withers. In obese horses, the withers will be bulging with fat.

Neck. In an extremely thin horse, you will be able to see the bone structure of the neck, and the throatlatch will be very trim. As the horse gains condition, fat is deposited down the top of the neck. A body condition score of 8 is characterized by a neck that is thick all around, with fat evident at the crest and the throatlatch.

Shoulder. As a horse gains weight, fat is deposited around the shoulder to help it blend smoothly with the body. As condition scores increase, fat is deposited behind the shoulder, especially in the region behind the elbow.

Something for your ride log: The "Ridgeway Trot" (CRI)

"The Ridgeway Trot." Sounds like a dance step, doesn't it? *Bow to your partner, bow to your corner, do-si-do and Ridgeway Trot!* But although the foxtrot and the turkey trot really *are* dance steps, the "Ridgeway Trot" is not.

Also known as the Cardiac Recovery Index (or CRI), the Ridgeway Trot is a tool that vets use to judge a horse's ability to recover from exercise. The technique was originally advocated by AERC Hall of Fame endurance rider and veterinarian Kerry Ridgeway, DVM, and the name stuck. You can do a CRI (or a Ridgeway Trot) on your horse at the mid-point and/or at the end of each training ride to track changes in fitness level.

The CRI is not much more complicated than a normal trot-out (see "Teaching the Trot-out" in Chapter 3). There are a just a few extra data-gathering steps so that you have a heart-rate measurement taken *before* a trot-out to compare with a measurement taken 60 seconds later.

Ideally, the two numbers are the same. If the pulse of the horse at each point is 60, the CRI score is recorded as 60/60.

In the case of a very fresh and/or very fit horse, the second number may be lower than the first. If the pulse of the horse was 60 bpm *before* the trot-out and 56 bpm *after* the trot-out, the CRI score is recorded as 60/56. This seems counterintuitive, but the movement of a fit horse actually moderately increases cooling of the skin and blood, which can result in a drop in heart rate.

If the pulse has *increased* after the trot-out, there is cause for concern. While a 4-beat increase (from 60 bpm to 64 bpm, for example) isn't alarming, an 8-beat or higher increase is fair warning that the horse might be too fatigued to continue in good health.

You want the information about your horse's level of fitness during a CRI exam to be as accurate as possible. For most horses, that means that the trot-out should be performed at a medium-slow jog, rather than a brisk run. This pace keeps him from overheating, and allows his heart rate to have dropped by the time you check it again.

When doing a CRI in front of a vet at an endurance ride, you won't have an opportunity to slosh water on your horse between the two pulse checks, so you want to avoid letting him build up steam, which will make his heart pump fast. You are permitted to verbally and physically soothe your horse by stroking his neck and asking him to lower his head. I like to *yawn* at my horse after we return to the vet. This physical motion relaxes me, and gives the horse the message that *nothing interesting is happening here, so stand still and relax for a bit.* Even fake yawning works—your body (and your horse) can't tell the difference

7.2: How to pulse a horse

Correct location to pulse a horse behind the front left leg.

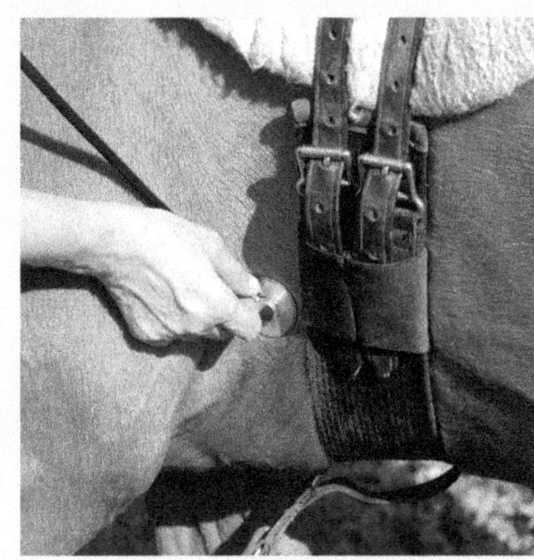

If necessary to help you hear clearly, ask the horse to move his left front leg slightly forward, and place your stethoscope behind the left front leg. You may have to practice a bit to find the right place. When you hear the steady lub-dub of the heartbeat, leave your stethoscope in place and look at your watch.

Listen for 15 seconds, counting each lub-dub as a single beat.

Multiply the number of beats by 4. This will give you the number of heart beats per minute. For example, 15 beats in a 15-second time span is a heart rate of 60 bpm; 14 beats in 15 seconds is 56 bpm; 13 beats in 15 seconds is 52 bpm, and so forth.

between a real yawn and a fake yawn—the process will slow your breathing and relax your muscles and this will cue your horse to relax with you.

(Do you yawn just reading the word "yawn"? I do!)

You also want to avoid stressing your horse emotionally between the two pulse checks. If your horse's best buddy has been beside you all day, and the buddy leaves to go to the water tank in the middle of your CRI exam, your horse may have an emotional meltdown—and his heart rate will skyrocket. Make a deal with your riding partner in advance to stick close together when the horses are being examined at a ride. Vets understand about buddy horses; as long as the buddy is standing quietly and not crowding anybody or making a fuss, nobody will mind having the two horses stand side-by-side while pulses are taken.

The CRI numbers should improve as the horse rests. For example, a horse with a 60/60 CRI score 10 minutes after exercise has ceased can be expected to show a better score (52/52, for example) after 10 or 15 additional minutes of rest.

By practicing the CRI at home at the end of your training sessions, you will familiarize your horse with the process. This will also make you familiar with his normal recovery numbers and times. Here's the process:

Take the pulse of the horse (see Sidebar 7.2: How to pulse a horse) at the beginning of the examination.

As soon as the pulse is recorded, start trotting. Start your stopwatch (my phone has a handy application for this; you can also use your watch) when you begin trotting. Take the horse out on a normal trot-out, which is approximately 125 feet out and 125 feet back (45 strides or so, each direction).

When 60 seconds have passed since the first pulse check, measure the heart rate of the horse again.

Compare the two measurements.

That's the Ridgeway Trot! *(Do-si-do optional).*

Endurance events depend on the combined efforts of trail crews, ride managers, volunteers and vets.

CHAPTER 8
VISIT A RIDECAMP WITHOUT YOUR HORSE

It is difficult for new riders to understand why experienced competitors recommend that they visit a ridecamp *without* a horse to observe—or better yet, volunteer—before leaping feet-first into participation in the sport.

Some newcomers may be shy about introducing themselves to a huge crowd of experienced participants. They may prefer to "slip in the back door" with their horse and quietly and unobtrusively enter the competition. Others are eager to play the game and don't want to waste time by spending a ride day hanging out at a vet check.

Yet, watching and helping will provide more knowledge than you could ever acquire by merely reading a book—even this book—or lurking on endurance listservs. Some things must be experienced in person to get their full benefit. This chapter offers advice about *why* and *how* you can come to camp without a horse, and details skills you can learn or sharpen while in camp without your horse.

Reasons to come to camp without your horse

There are certain advantages to making your first visit or two to ridecamp horseless.

You can observe *everything* going on around you without having to filter your observations through the lens of "what is my horse going to think of *this?*" The variety and level of equestrian activity may surprise you… and some surprises are better when they are *not* shared with a 1000-pound prey animal.

Unencumbered by your horse, you will have time to make yourself known to the ride manager (RM) and some veterinarians and will also have the opportunity to meet volunteers skilled in the arts of pulsing, timing, and water tank filling. You will have the chance to meet many other riders, too—something you might not have time to do otherwise. These people are important. They are also potential new friends.

Give riders, crews, and everyone else your undivided attention. People you've admired online may be different in real life; people who keep a low profile on listservs may shine and offer useful skills.

Watch and learn. A person who comes to a ride with an open mind and two unbroken arms has the opportunity to learn and practice skills that will be *very* useful, including trail marking/unmarking, pulsing, and timing. Volunteer. If you want to brush up on vet-check skills, scribe for a vet. Most vets will teach their scribes as they go through the day, and you will gain valuable skills in caring for your horse when you begin to compete.

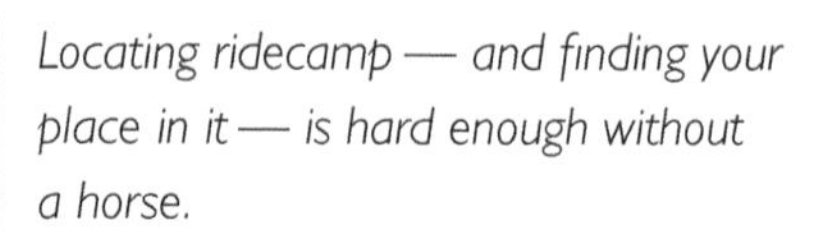

Locating ridecamp — and finding your place in it — is hard enough without a horse.

How to get the most of your horseless ridecamp experience

Come as early as possible before the ride. If the start time is Saturday at 6 a.m., try to arrive by noon on Friday. Touch base with the RM in advance to let her know that you are new, are willing to be put to work, and want to learn. But if your time is short and you can only come for a few hours on ride day, come anyway! You will meet people and learn stuff. You'll be glad you came.

When you arrive, check with ride management before you park and set up your sleeping quarters—they may have suggestions for you, like what spots are out of the "runaway horse" zone and away from the worst noise or mosquito zones.

Set up your living quarters, introduce yourself to neighbors, and take a walk around camp. Take mental (or written, or photographic) notes about what you see. What camping arrangements seem innovative and useful to you? What kinds of setups do you want to emulate or avoid when you bring your horse to camp? What food smells good enough that you might want to prepare it for yourself someday (alternately, which camps look friendly enough to invite you in for supper?)

Strike up conversations and ask questions. A good conversation starter can be "What a beautiful horse! How old is he?" There isn't an endurance rider alive who doesn't want to talk about horses.

When you have your bearings, go back to ride management headquarters and offer to help. If they need help with a task you aren't prepared to do, ask to be taught. Most useful ridecamp skills can be taught in 15 minutes (or less), but practice makes everything easier; lots of practice sharpens skills.

Tasks that need doing, skills you might learn

Pre-ride tasks

Printing numbers on horses. This involves a large grease marker and requires the skill to draw on a wiggly, furry surface. Ride numbers are printed on the rider's vet card. The number is then drawn on one or both of the horse's hips. If the horse is a kicker, it's okay to hold the lead rope and ask the owner/rider to draw the number.

Benny stands quietly for his number, applied by a first-time volunteer.

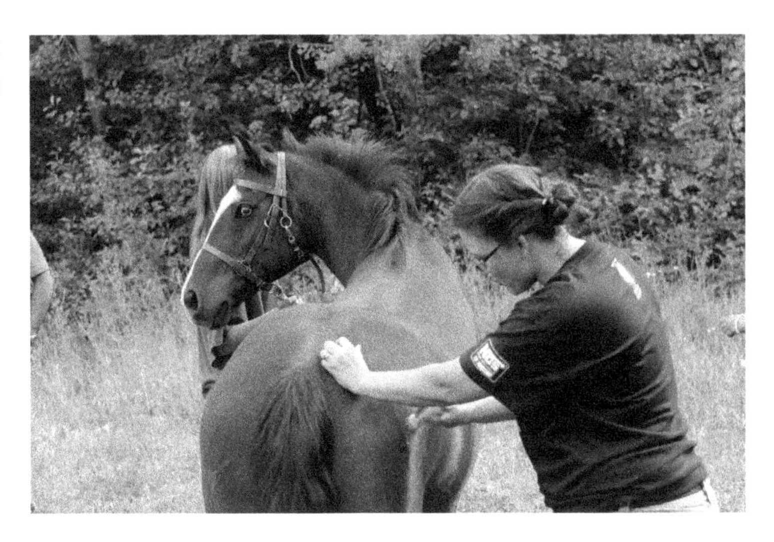

Pulsing horses. See Chapter 7's sidebar for pulsing directions, or ask somebody to show you how to do it. Pulsing a field full of horses will not only strengthen your pulsing skills, it will also give you an auditory window into the reality of endurance horse behavior. It is amazing how many horses that appear to be completely witless with excitement are actually quite calm and exhibit a low standing pulse.

Veterinary scribing. The vet examines each horse for approximately 3 minutes per animal, checking set parameters (see Chapter 11 for more details about veterinary criteria) and grading each parameter: A (superior), B (acceptable), C (cause for concern), or D (unacceptable and cause for elimination). A veterinary scribe records each of the grades on the ride card, and is also in a position to listen to conversations and discussions between veterinarians and between riders and specific vets. Vet scribes are in a position to learn a *lot* in a very short time period.

Gophering. A gopher ("go-fer") assists the RM or any of the ride management team in coping with the major or minor disasters that inevitably crop up at the last minute. From troubleshooting the computer database to finding fresh gasoline for a generator, whatever skills you have will be useful to somebody. If ride management has everything under control, they may ask you to assist a specific rider who needs an extra set of hands.

Ride-day tasks

Checking rider numbers on rider cards as they leave camp or enter and leave vet checks. You may be asked to record the time of day on rider cards or statistic sheets.

Pulsing horses. Pulses are checked again when horses enter a vet check. Once a horse's pulse drops to the established criteria (generally 60-64 bpm), the horse is "down" and this information must be communicated—usually by hollering—to the ride timer.

Assisting the timer. Help to keep track of shouted numbers, times, and whatever else needs to be tracked.

Scribing for the vet. Vets will examine horses quickly but thoroughly on ride day. A vet scribe will see a lot of horses trot-out in the course of a day, and can learn a lot about spotting lameness in a horse.

Trotting out horses. As riders tire, it's nice to have a set of fresher feet to trot the horse for the vet exam. If this is new to you, ask for directions (and see Chapter 3).

Water tank filling. A camp full of horses uses an astonishing amount of water in a single day, and it is vital that tanks on the ride course and in camp be kept full. This is time consuming and often underappreciated. And once you do it for a day, you will never approach a water tank without breathing a word of thanks to the volunteers who put it there and keep it filled for your use.

Pulse-checking happens at several points during the ride, so it is a very valuable skill.

Feeding volunteers and vets. Somebody somewhere in each camp makes sandwiches and snacks to keep the volunteers metabolically stable. That person could be you.

Gophering. As above—doing everything that needs to be done, at top speed.

Post-ride volunteer opportunities

Unmarking the trail. Taking a trail apart generally happens much faster than putting it together. Volunteers cover the trail on quads, trucks, bicycles, or horses to pull ribbons, take down signs and pie-plate markers, and scuff out messages written in paint or lime powder.

Dumping and collecting water tanks.

Cleaning up camp. From collecting garbage to scooping manure into trash bags, the ridecamp must be returned to a state of tidiness before ride management goes home. Riders are often very helpful, but volunteers are useful in making sure it all gets done.

After just one weekend as a ride volunteer and observer, you will have a much clearer notion about how an endurance ride runs from start to finish. You'll have a better idea of how prepared you are and can identify training and gear that you want to secure before coming to camp again. And next time, bring the horse!

Decisions, decisions: what to pack, who bunks with whom, what to wear, what about crew?

CHAPTER 9
ALMOST READY FOR YOUR FIRST RIDE

Your horse is getting fit and you are getting excited. You visit the AERC.org website and check the calendar: There's a ride that you can attend! It's only two months away…

Eeeeeek!

This chapter includes a bare-bones calendar of tasks you'll want to do before ride day, arranged in a countdown format. The schedule isn't set in stone, but it is a handy list of stuff to remember. This chapter also contains packing suggestions and advice about items you will need for camping with your horse, as well as some of the "unwritten rules" of ridecamp. Finally, there are a few words from the Bad Idea Fairy.

Countdown to the first ride

Ride day minus 2 months

- Check the fit of your saddle and make necessary adjustments.
- Take a riding lesson (on trails, if possible). Ask your instructor to focus on helping you and your horse move freely and comfortably at various speeds over different terrain.
- Call your farrier to set a farrier appointment for 1-2 weeks before the event.
- Administer any needed vaccinations.
- Ask your vet about medical paperwork that may be required for the ride. If you need to cross state lines for your event, be sure to alert your vet so that the paperwork can be ready in time.

Ride day minus 1 month

- Safety-check your rig: tires (check your spare tire, too), wiring, brakes, floorboards. Fix anything that needs fixing.
- Write down your tire information. If anything is likely to die on the road, it will be a tire. What size/grade tire do you have on your trailer (and truck)? What PSI do your tires require? Having the spouse/mechanic look stuff over is good, but having the information handy in the glove box is better. Know that trailer tires are *not the same* as truck tires of the same size. They are built differently. If the place you call in an emergency doesn't know the difference

or insists that truck tires are adequate, call another place. Write this information on a piece of paper and store it somewhere safe.

- Evaluate your camping gear. Check out your camping arrangements and think ahead. Do your sleeping quarters leak? Do you know how to set up in windy or rainy conditions? Does your camp stove work, and do you have fresh fuel? Repair or replace anything that might fail in camp.
- Practice administering electrolytes to your horse via syringe. Start with a diluted dose mixed with applesauce or yogurt. If your horse does not take the syringe quietly, start teaching him now to accept it.

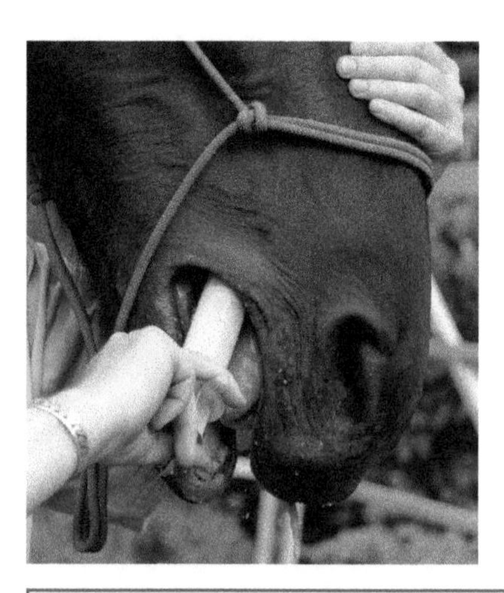

Practice syringing with something yummy.

9.1: Electrolytes

What are electrolytes and does your horse need them?

Electrolytes are, simply, salts. These salts occur naturally in a horse's diet and are supplemented by a salt block, loose salt added to the feed, or a concentrated electrolyte mixture administered to a horse who is working hard. The science on equine athletic electrolytes is inexact. Just as some human athletes cannot perform well without drinking their weight in Gatorade™, it appears that many endurance horses perform better and recover faster from exertion if they receive electrolyte supplements.

Not all horses need electrolytes, especially for a shorter event (less than 50 miles) in temperate conditions (55 degrees, breezy with light rain) over non-complicated terrain (firm footing, minimal changes in altitude). Ask yourself if your horse will eat and drink on the trail on his own. Does he accept a syringe willingly? Does administering electrolytes encourage him to drink, or do they make him stick out his tongue at you and stop eating in protest over the flavor? Test his reactions to electrolytes when you have a long training ride at home and watch to see if his heart rate stays lower, if he drinks more water, or if he refuses to eat grass along the trail after being syringed with the salty stuff (Stuart, 2008).

In an unpublished study of Tevis competitors by Garlinghouse, blood samples analyzed at the finish line showed that horses supplemented with small, frequent doses of electrolytes during the event consistently showed a faster and more complete recovery. Horses supplemented only at vet checks (every 2-3 hours) were slower to recover. Horses supplemented infrequently or not at all during the event recovered the slowest.

Based on Garlinghouse's study, it is evident that small doses of electrolytes administered frequently can be beneficial. But as with many aspects of endurance riding, the product(s) used, the amount administered, and the method of administration are left to the rider, and results may vary based on these factors.

To offset what some horses may find to be a bad taste and to avoid ulceration in the mouth caused by concentrated raw salt, riders often mix electrolytes with a buffering agent such as applesauce or yogurt. Alternately, you may wish to mix electrolyte powder with your horse's food, but only if your horse will eat it. If your horse steadfastly picks around the salty bits, or turns up his nose entirely at electrolyte-enhanced food, you will need to try something else.

Ride day minus 2 weeks

- Optimally, farrier work is performed 2 weeks prior to the ride.
- If you need to make any feed changes for the event (switching from your usual feed to weed-free hay, for example) start making those changes gradually 2 weeks before you leave home.
- Test the arrangements that you will use to contain your horse in camp. Keep your horse in it at least overnight, and preferably for 2 or 3 nights.
- Check that your paperwork is current and stored in the rig: horse's health papers, vehicle papers, etc. If you need a short-term health certificate from your vet, get it now. If you will travel with another horse, get paperwork for him, too.
- Make a list of emergency contacts to use while on the road. The list should contain phone numbers for roadside assistance and a veterinary hospital in the area of your destination, as well as emergency contact information for you and every person and animal travelling with you.

Ride day minus 1 week

- Load your trailer with horse feed and tack.

If there is an out-check planned at the ride you will need a bag, tub, or bucket for your gear. Chose something you can seal up tightly and label clearly.

Ride day minus 2 days

- Pack your own gear: clothing for ride day, stuff for camp, and clean clothing (and shoes) for travelling. Check the weather forecast and plan your wardrobe accordingly... but bring extra sunscreen and extra rain gear just in case the forecast is wrong. It's never a bad idea to bring extra socks.
- Purchase and pack groceries for the people in your group.
- If you are planning to use electrolytes, give your horse electrolytes prior to leaving home, preferably the evening before you leave, and again in the morning before you load up. This will encourage drinking before the journey begins. If you plan to use electrolytes during the ride, pre-mix them into syringes at home. Seal the syringe ends with duct tape and store them in a large Ziploc bag for convenience.
- Make sure you have directions to camp. Check road conditions if travelling through a city, over a mountain pass, or any other place where problems might occur. I print out everything and leave it all on the dashboard of my truck. DO NOT DEPEND ON YOUR VEHICLE GPS. GPS signals are often weak in wilderness areas.
- Some people leave home 2 days before the event, which is nice but not necessary unless the travel is extensive.

Ride day minus 1 day

- Pack up and go!
- On the way, hit the ATM. Cash is preferred when paying for ride photos, tack, and emergency hoof care.
- When travelling, stop every 3-4 hours for 15-20 minutes (or more). Fuel stops count as rest stops—while your rig is filling up, offer water, plus carrots or soaked beet pulp to your horse. My horses travel with hay bags in the trailer, so they can munch as we drive. If travelling in very hot conditions, consider driving at night or in the very early morning to minimize heat stress for the horses.
- Another tip for travelling in hot weather: set up a manger in the trailer and place a pan of very sloppy beet pulp in it for your horse to eat on the road, so that he can maintain his hydration as you travel.

Choose your distance: novice ride or LD or 50 miler?

Some experienced endurance riders like to say that they never start a new horse on less than a 50 miler, because they want the horse to grok early on the significance of the work he is being asked to do, and that may be a good choice for those people, since they already know a lot about the sport.

However, if you're reading this book, chances are good that you are at an earlier stage of the learning curve. Appropriate goals for yourself at your first event might include

- Stay on course
- Find an all-day pace and stick with it
- Complete the ride with a happy, healthy horse
- Finish within the allowed time
- Have fun

Goal for every ride: have fun!

Appropriate goals for your horse at the first event may include

- Remain responsive to the rider through the excitement of the start
- Move down the trail at a reasonable, ratable speed
- Make good choices about gait/speed for the terrain

- Eat when offered food, drink when offered water
- Behave properly for vets and pulsers
- Have fun

For most new distance riders, the limited distance (25-35 miles) or the novice ride (8-15 miles; sometimes also called the "fun ride") are better choices than a 50 miler, even if your horse is very fit. The first ride is a huge learning experience, and it's difficult for the brain to learn stuff when the body is tired. For more details about fatigue, see the section about DIMR in Chapter 11.

Choose a distance that will allow you and your horse to succeed and learn. If you are undecided, talk to the ride manager or a rider who is familiar with the event—she will be able to tell you more about the terrain and ride conditions, and the extra information will help you make a smart choice.

This is a useful system for storing things you might need in a hurry.

What to pack for your horse

Start by packing the equipment you use every day.

Buckets. At minimum, you will want a water bucket, a bucket or pan for grain and/or mash, and an extra bucket because if you don't have an extra bucket you will need it for some crazy thing but if you do have an extra bucket you can just use it as a step-stool all weekend. The water bucket should be the largest bucket you can bring; big buckets are less likely to tip over.

Grooming tools. Some basic brushes, a hoof pick, and a mane comb. If your horse's mane is thick, long, or heavy, bring some rubber bands and be ready to braid it the night before the ride so that you can keep him cooler (see Chapter 11: Keeping warm and keeping cool).

Feed and water. Horses in camp will have minimal opportunity to graze, so if your horse is pastured at home, he will need a *lot* more feed in camp than you usually provide at home. Hay bales can be carried in hay bags or wrapped in tarps. Beet pulp can travel in a large bucket with a lid or in an unopened bag from the feed store. Grain and supplements can be premeasured into Ziploc bags for convenient use in camp. If your horse trailer has a water tank on board, fill it. If it doesn't, consider carrying at least 20 gallons of water in buckets with lids. A huge bag of carrots or apples will be welcomed by your equine friends and will encourage them to eat while surrounded by the distractions of camp.

A blanket. Even horses who are normally not blanketed at home may appreciate an extra layer of warmth, especially if camp is at a higher altitude or if the weather rolls in. The blanket will also keep fatigued muscles warm after the ride.

A wool or fleece cooler. A cooler can be taken to the vet check to keep your horse's hard-working muscles warm if the wind is cold or the rain blows in. It can also be wrapped around a chilly rider if the horse seems sufficiently warm, or be used to keep the bugs at bay if those are problematic in camp.

Functionality is more important than fashion... even for the horses.

Bug spray. Speaking of bugs, bring fly spray, a fly sheet, or yellow-jacket traps if the ride literature mentions any kind of insect. There's nothing as bothersome to a weary horse as biting bugs.

Tack. Clean it up before you pack it, *but don't change anything.* The day of the ride is the worst time to try anything new. Stick with whatever has worked for you in the past, even if it's old, ugly, or a strange color. Double-check to make sure you've got everything.

To this stack of stuff, add a few things you mostly need only in ridecamp.

- Electrolytes and syringes (see Sidebar 9.1).
- A box or bag of stuff to take to the vet check(s). If you don't have a special crew bag, Rubbermaid boxes work well, or you can use a bucket with a lid.
- A few big, heavy-duty trash bags—useful if you are asked to pack out your manure, otherwise just useful to have.
- A huge scrubby sponge and a squeegee are great for a quick rinse. Bring poultice clay and paper if you intend to poultice legs after the ride or ice boots if you intend to use them.

With practice, packing gets easier. If necessary, make yourself a list of "must-have" items and use it as a master packing list.

Horse containment systems in camp

There are several options for containing your horse in camp. Whichever one you choose, practice using it *at home* before coming to camp. You want to be completely comfortable setting up the containment system once you're in camp, and you want to be sure that your horse isn't going to bust out of it and get lost in the hills for 4 days.

9.2: You don't want to lose a horse

When I started riding endurance, I rode Story, who could be contained in a fence made of masking tape. We used an electric tape fence connected to a charger run on a bunch of D-cell batteries. No worries.

A few years later, I brought the Toad and put him in the electric tape fence. He was nervous about being away from home for the first time, but he was parked next to his buddy and a pile of hay, so all was well... at first

Around 11 p.m., a mare in the camp next to us saw a ghost (or a leaf... or a piece of paper... or an air molecule...) and slammed into her PVC-pipe corral. The night was cold, and the cold plastic exploded like a beer bottle in a blender. The mare ran towards our horses, and they ran away from her, dragging the electric tape behind their scared selves.

The good news is that they were in a fenced enclosure. The bad news is that the enclosure was the size of my hometown.

Our horses were gone. Gone. For 4 days, they were GONE.

I assure you that you *never* want to find yourself hitching up an empty trailer for the drive home like we did.

Our horses were eventually located by cowboys on quads who found them while moving cattle, and they came home not much worse for wear. However, that ended the years of containing *those* horses with electric tape.

Tie the horse to the trailer. This option has the advantage of being cheap and familiar to most horses and riders. Disadvantages include limiting the horse's ability to move around, roll, or lay down to sleep. Be prepared to walk your horse around camp frequently to stretch his legs if you choose this option. If you sleep inside the horse trailer, you will curse the horse's movement every time he bumps his hay bag against the wall of the trailer or bangs his nose against the bucket propped up on the fender. If your horse pulls back against the rope, consider tying him with TWO ropes—one short (which may break) and one longer (which will hopefully restrain your horse after he breaks the first rope).

A horse "docking" system. Products such as the HiTie™ or Springtie™ systems use a docking system originally designed to keep large boats tied to docks in port. An overhead rod attaches securely to the side of the trailer allowing the horse a large space to move around in. The rod is flexible enough to allow the horse to roll or lay down to sleep. Disadvantages include a lack of protection for your horse from "incoming" hazards, such as dogs or horses that have gotten loose from other camps. If your horse is a hussy like mine or has a nasty attitude towards intruders, this is not a good option.

There is no "perfect" horse containment system. Use what works best for your horse.

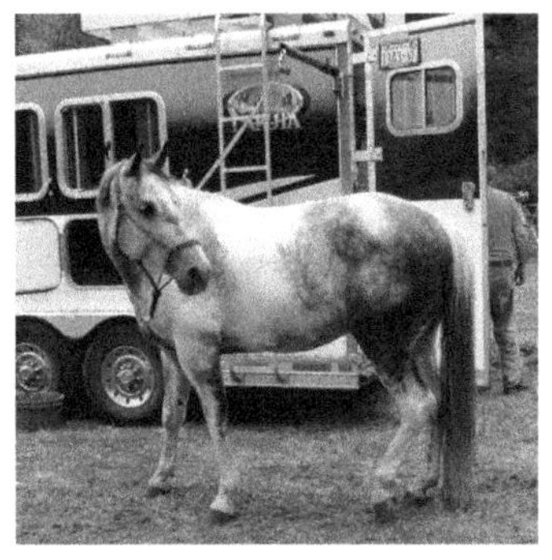

Electric corrals. If your horse is accustomed to (and respectful of) electric tape fencing or cross fencing at home, building a small tape corral in camp may be a good option for him. Electric tape is lightweight, flexible in shape, and easy to assemble. The disadvantage to this option is that a horse wearing a blanket may not feel the electric jolt and might therefore not respect the barrier. A frightened horse may run right through an electric tape fence and end up far away. Battery failures are common.

Portable corral panels. Some corrals are lightweight, tall enough to discourage jumping, and a good visual and physical barrier. Other corrals are sturdy enough to keep the animal contained, but each section can weigh 50 pounds or more. Make sure ahead of time that the pieces are light enough for you to set them up in the dark, in the rain, by yourself. Rails should be far apart enough that a hoof will not get caught, and narrow enough that a head won't fit partway and get stuck. If your horse is inclined to challenge his surroundings, opt for the heavier option, and make sure the connecting hardware is also sturdy.

To summarize, when choosing a horse containment system:

- Know your horse.
- Remember that both visual *and* physical barriers are important.
- Sturdiness is important in a corral, but if it's too heavy, you will hate it. That said, get something sturdier than you need—not all the problems come from inside the corral.

9.3: Horse ID Tags

I hope your horse is never lost like mine was.

However, just in case the unthinkable happens, make him easier to "get found" by purchasing a dog tag, luggage tag, or similar item engraved with the horse's name and your basic contact information (cell phone number, license plate number of your truck).

Braid the tag into your horse's mane or tail. A shoelace, sturdy string, or pipe cleaner works nicely to keep the tag in place and visible..

What to pack for the rider

Here's my suggested packing list:

Clothing. Stuff you have pre-tested *in training* for ride day (see Chapter 2 for details about riding clothes). Clothes for both the day before and the day after the ride, and possibly, clean shoes for travelling. The morale-boosting power of clean socks cannot be understated. Even if you normally travel with nothing but the bare essentials, bring two extra pairs of clean, warm, dry socks to camp. You can thank me later.

Sleeping/relaxing clothes. No matter how little you wear at home, in camp you will be happier sleeping in a t-shirt and sweatpants. Because if you don't, your horse is going to escape, and you'll have to scramble for clothes before you go after him, or risk bug bites and humiliation as you chase after him naked.

Shoes and boots as needed for the weather and terrain.

Outerwear appropriate to the weather forecast, plus a warmer/dryer layer in case the forecast is completely wrong.

Food. (See sections below.) Remember to take pots, pans, utensils, and a can opener! A cooler is useful. So is an insulated lunch bag, if you plan to pack chilled food for your lunch at an out-vet check. Check your cooking set up to make sure you have sufficient stove fuel and at least one pancake-flipper type tool. Bring water to drink and wash with: horse water is routinely provided by ride management, but potable water is often a luxury.

Sleeping quarters. This can be as simple as a sleeping bag in the bed of a truck or as complex as a Living Quarters (LQ) section of a fancy horse trailer. Whatever you use, check it for leaks before you go.

Hygiene and medical kit. Bring toothbrush, toothpaste, and any necessary medications. Remember sunscreen, Benadryl, and painkillers (if you think you might be a bit sore at the finish line). Ladies: it is never a bad idea to pack feminine hygiene products, even if you think you won't need them. They can also be used as horse-bandaging materials in an emergency.

Towel. Because you are a hoopy frood who always knows the location of your towel.

No matter what your sleeping quarters are, check for leaks before you leave home.

What to pack for friends and crew who come to camp with you

Assume that your friends are basically competent people who will bring their own toothbrushes; however it's wise to treat with kindness anyone who consents to come to camp as your crew. For these blessed individuals, pack an extra camp chair and an assortment of tasty snacks and beverages. More details on making your crew feel valued are available in Chapter 10.

Hand your friends a copy of this book as well—they can brush up on their crewing skills by reading it while they wait for you at a vet check.

Foods that work, foods to avoid, and hydration

Endurance is *hard work*. To finish your event, you need every scrap of extra energy and every single grey cell the Almighty left in your custody. Your horse is depending on you to take care of yourself so that you can make good decisions on his behalf.

Water. The most important food is *water*. Your mental acuity can be affected at as little as 1% dehydration, and not in a good way. At 2%, your aerobic endurance performance is reduced and is further exacerbated if you continue to exercise in a hot environment. Dehydration doesn't just impair your reflexes and gross motor skills; it directly affects your ability to think and to stay alert and YOU ARE GOING TO NEED ALL THAT STUFF on the endurance trail!

See the sidebar about DIMR in Chapter 11 for more information about dehydration.

Sports drinks aren't necessary unless you are exercising hard in an environment much hotter than your normal training conditions offer, or unless you are extremely sensitive to heat. If the flavor of sports drinks will encourage you to drink more fluids, consider splitting an 8-ounce sports drink between four large water bottles and topping them up with water. Most sports drinks contain a bunch of sugars that can cause a severe boink when they wear off, which might really suck if you are still an hour or two away from the vet check. *Never* try out a new sports drink at a ride (that is the voice of experience).

So, drink your water. Start consuming extra fluids 2 days before the ride if possible. I understand that this makes driving long distances a bit awkward. Consider, however, that your pit stops are also brief breaks for the horses in the trailer, and that's a good thing. Remember that if you aren't peeing, you aren't drinking enough fluids.

Drink your water. Drink your water. Drink your water.

Food. Every rider is different and has different preferences and needs during a ride weekend. But here are some general guidelines to keep in mind. On the evening before the ride, I strongly advise you to avoid excess alcohol (which contributes to dehydration, among other things) and carbonated beverages (because those bubbles are *really* unwelcome on the first leg of a ride when the horses are all fizzy).

Other foods to avoid include chili and anything spicy. My friend Aimee and I were *very* glad that we had only signed up to ride a LD event the day after we snacked our way through a large bag of dried gourmet wasabi peas. Save the gumbo, the greasy sausage, the extra-spicy Thai food, and the coconut rum drinks for your meal *after* the ride.

Prior to the ride, I recommend that you eat plenty of protein and crunchy veggies and fruit, and drink lots of water. Choose salty chips or nuts to encourage yourself to drink water.

If you suffer from a nervous tummy before the ride (common), good foods for breakfast include oatmeal, applesauce, yogurt, a banana or an apple. Otherwise, your normal breakfast food is fine.

Vet-check and lunch-stop foods that travel well and taste good include V8® juice (an excellent source of electrolytes), other juices, fresh fruit, yogurt, string cheese, peanut butter sandwiches, and salty chips. Some riders swear by meal drinks such as Ensure™ and SlimFast™.

Trail food can include granola, nuts, and commercial energy bars such as BellyTimber™ or PowerBars™. A handful of cough drops or individually wrapped candies are nice throat soothers on a dusty trail.

Choose food that is easy to chew, swallow, and digest—preferably something that won't turn disgusting if it gets hot or squashed.

Consider "decaffeinating" yourself the week before a ride. It's difficult to choke down a huge mug of coffee before the start line, and the headache at mile 7 can be unbelievable if you are accustomed to a big dose of caffeine each morning.

After the ride, many riders are hungry for

PROTEIN! Meat, cheese, and beans are really welcome after a long day on the trail.
FLAVOR! Now is the time to break out the Cajun spices, the Thai soup mix, and the garlic.
CRUNCH! Celery, fresh snap peas, and broccoli are welcome after the easily-chewed foods you've focused on all day.
WATER. Drink it.

For your first few rides, pack a variety of foods to eat in camp before and after the ride, and a wide variety of stuff that you think might appeal to you at vet checks. Don't forget that you will get *tired*—and cooking and eating will seem like hard work to a tired rider. Carefully avoid foods associated with allergies or sensitivities—the excitement and exercise may make reactions more severe.

Keep track of what you eat and what you don't. I pitch all the food trash back into a cooler, and then take notes about which packages and peelings are empty at the end of a weekend so I can figure out which foods I actually ate and which foods I ignored during the event. The list of "foods eaten" becomes the shopping list for the next event.

Ride meeting is just one of the many uses you'll find for your chair.

The unwritten "rules" of ridecamp

A ridecamp is full of friendly people with common values and goals. However, when people in camp get tired they can become cranky. Keep the following tips in mind:

- If you are confused about how something is done, ask! Find the vet or the manager or an experienced rider who doesn't seem too busy.
- Be as courteous as you can—good advice anywhere.
- Keep your dog on a leash. Even if he's the nicest dog in the world, there will be somebody in camp who won't like him or, worse yet, a horse who will try to stomp him. If your dog cannot stand to be on a leash or tied to your trailer, leave him home.
- If your rig has a generator, obey the camp guidelines for quiet times. This includes *really quiet* generators. Turn it off by 10 p.m., regardless, so that the engine noise and fumes don't disturb others.
- If your horse kicks, bites, or "doesn't like to be touched there," flag his tail with a red ribbon. If your horse is not a Good Citizen, be vigilant about keeping him away from other horses in camp, on the trail, and in the vet lines.
- Stallions are welcome in camp… as long as nobody can *tell* they're stallions! If Studly has trouble containing his hormones, leave him at home and work on his training until he can behave politely in a crowd.
- No matter where you are, keep space between yourself and other horses. It's always possible that a horse HAD a red-flagged tail, but the flag got lost somewhere. Stay safe, leave room.
- Don't take all the free stuff: water, hay, ice, food, or whatever. Leave some for the next horse and rider.
- If somebody needs help and you have a free moment, offer to assist.
- At the ride meeting, take notes and listen carefully. Save questions for the end.

And remember, if you are confused, ask!

The Bad Idea Fairy's ridecamp packing list

Margarita mix and a blender. Because the salt on the rim counts as electrolyting, right? And extra tequila—you can never have too much tequila. Chili for dinner sounds good before the ride--it will go great with the margaritas!

One pair of shoes—I only have one pair of feet, so one pair of shoes is plenty.

I will pack ***just enough*** *of everything—just enough people food, just enough hay, just enough forks and cups and socks. Margins of error are for losers who make mistakes, and I'm a winner!*

Printing directions is a waste of paper. I can pull up the ride info on my smartphone at any time!

Alarm clocks take up valuable space, and I'll be too excited to oversleep.

Bringing cash is an invitation to thieves and writing checks is for old ladies. There's bound to be a cash machine in camp, right?

My horse doesn't need a blanket in summer, ***duh!*** *Save that space in the trailer and bring a stack of DVDs to watch on my laptop instead.*

There's no place quite as pretty as a ridecamp…

especially after a long day on the trail!.

CHAPTER 10
THE FIRST RIDE, PART ONE

As you top the hill that overlooks the ridecamp, you will see more horse rigs than you've ever imagined in one place convened out in the middle of nowhere. Maybe that's when the tummy butterflies take flight. Or maybe they start fluttering when you are trying on your calm, been-there-done-that look as you back your rig into your selected spot… and then pull forward and back again… and then pull forward and back again....

Your first time at a ridecamp can be overwhelmingly strange and confusing. This chapter will give you an idea of what to expect and provide tips to help the experience go more smoothly. It also gives you advice on working well with a crew if you are lucky enough to have one.

Timetable: What happens when

Parking and setting up

Try to arrive early in the day. There will be times when you simply cannot arrive in camp before dark, but for your first time it will be much easier if you arrive in mid-afternoon so you can see the layout and organization of the camp in daylight.

If there seems to be a rhyme or reason to the parking, try to follow it. Otherwise, situate yourself as close to a water tank and/or a Porta-Potty as possible.

Leave your horse inside the trailer or tied outside the trailer while you set up your horse containment. When your horse containment is ready with feed and water buckets full, put him in it. If necessary, keep your lead rope on him and in your hand for a few minutes if he seems excessively nervous while looking at his new surroundings. Once he buries his face in the hay, continue with your camp set up.

A folding cart or wheelbarrow is handy for toting gear.

Set up your own sleeping quarters. Be ready for curious neighbors (humans and dogs, mostly) to come by and say hello. If you are willing to talk to people, camp set up can take longer because of all the chatting, but you'll have plenty of help. I like to orient my sleeping quarters so that I can point a flashlight at my horse to check on her without getting all the way out of bed.

If there will be an out-vet check, set up a box or bag of supplies. If you will be giving your horse electrolytes during the event, send electrolytes out to the vet check in syringes sealed with duct tape.

Signing up and vetting in

When you are feeling organized—and while the sun is still up—visit the ridecamp office and sign in. Bring your AERC card with you (a surcharge applies to non-members) plus your horse's breed registration information.

At registration, you will complete forms and hand over money in return for a rider information packet, which usually includes a vet card (also called a "ride card" or "rider card"), a rider number, and information about the ride and the trail. Keep track of all that stuff!

After you have registered, you are ready to take your horse to the vet check. If he's spent a long day in the trailer, walk him around camp for at least 20 minutes to allow him to stretch his legs and eat some grass, or saddle up and take a short ride. Visit every water tank in camp before taking him to the vet check for the in-check so he has plenty of opportunities to drink water and look around.

At the in-check a Pulse and Respiration volunteer ("pulser") will use a stethoscope to take your horse's pulse. Assist her by having your horse stand still. You may have to move his left front foot forward slightly to allow better access—make sure ahead of time that he is comfortable with this action. Have your vet card ready so the pulser can write on it. Don't worry if your horse's pulse is high (50 bpm or more) at the in-check; there's a lot of excitement around him, so a higher heart rate is normal.

A volunteer will write your ride number on your horse's hip using a grease marker. Ask your horse to stand still for this as well. If your horse is a kicker, ask the volunteer to hold his head while *you* mark the number on his bum.

When it's your turn to see the vet, hand your vet card over to the vet. *Tell the vet that you are new and ask for advice.* Most vets will take extra time with newcomers, explaining what they are checking for and what they hope to see. (Read more detailed information about the vet check in Chapter 11.) Hopefully, you have already taught your horse to do a trot-out (Chapter 3 contains instructions) because this is always part of the vet exam.

After the vet check, take your horse back to your camp and make sure he has plenty of food and water.

Prepare dinner and eat. Remember to minimize gassy and spicy foods! See Chapter 9 for suggestions on what to cook and eat.

While waiting in line for the vet, allow lots of room between horses, especially if one has a red "kicker" ribbon in its tail.

Get things organized for ride day. Make sure your saddle packs are ready, your water bottles are full, and everything you will want in the morning is easy to locate. If you boot your horse for a ride, put his boots on the night before—it will be much easier to do it in the quiet evening than in the morning when he's excited and dancing around. No need to snug up the gaiters; you can do that in the morning.

Socialize! When meeting new people in camp, a good ice breaker is "Your horse is lovely! What's his/her name?"

Ride meeting, bedtime, and night

When you go to the ride meeting, take your rider packet and a pen or pencil with you. Sit near the front and take notes. Save questions for the end and listen carefully. Points to listen for are location of water, special trail hazards and landmarks, and time cut-offs —including the start time! If the ride manager or vet offers to meet with new riders after the main meeting, attend the meeting.

After the ride meeting, put your camp to bed. Walk your horse around briefly if you like, and throw him an extra flake of hay—you want him to have enough food to last through the night. If you intend to administer electrolytes, wait until a few minutes after he's stopped eating before syringing them into his mouth. Follow this with a syringe full of water to rinse the extra salt out.

If there will be an out-vet check, take your crew bag or box of supplies to the designated spot so that it can be hauled out for you.

Experienced riders ask questions at the ride meeting because getting lost could mean missing a completion.

Settle down for the night. I keep a flashlight under my pillow so that I don't have to hunt for it when I need to get up in the night. I often sleep in my ride clothes, with sweats or fleece layers over the top if the weather is cold. If you don't want to sleep in ride clothes, set them out where they will be easy to grab in the morning.

Sidebar 10.1: What to send to the vet check

Remember that weary ride volunteers will be hefting and stacking your box or bag for transport to an out-check, so do them a favor and don't pack a bag or box heavier than 30 pounds. If your crew bag weighs more than a full bucket of water, split the supplies into two containers.

Things to include in your crew bag or box:

Horse feed. If ride management provides hay and/or alfalfa, you won't need to take this; otherwise, bring a flake or two. I also pack a gallon-size Ziploc bag of wet beet pulp, and other Ziplocs containing oats, grain, carrots, and apples. I won't necessarily feed everything to my horse, but if she's feeling picky I want to have a variety of feeds to tempt her appetite.

A feed pan—plastic or collapsible.

A lightweight fleece or wool horse blanket. This can be draped on the horse in cold weather or wrapped around a chilly rider (or crew person).

Electrolytes in syringes. Secure the tips with duct tape so they don't leak.

An extra lead rope.

A small tack repair kit. Duct tape, zip (cable) ties, a medium-sized carabiner, a scissor-snap or two, some shoelaces, a hoof boot.

A small medical kit. Ziploc bags containing sunscreen, Desitin®, Benadryl, baby wipes, bug spray, and any medications that might be wanted, plus a few Band-Aids of varying sizes.

Food for the rider. A sandwich, power bars, fruit juice or V8, string cheese, yogurt, and salty chips. If the weather is very hot, wrap a few horse ice boots around the food and pack it into a separate small cooler.

Water, to drink at the vet check and to take along for the next loop

Clothing for the rider, which can include pocket-sized raingear (or a large extra-strength trash bag to use as a rain poncho), a change of socks, a warm wool or fleece shirt, and a cooler cotton shirt. If you have room to send only one item of clothing, make that item *clean, dry* socks.

Things NOT to pack in your crew bag:

Extra set of horseshoes. Fizzy drinks. Chocolate stored in the same Ziploc as the clean socks. Food that will spoil. Food that takes longer than a few minutes to chew. Small dogs. Anything tremendously valuable. Anything breakable. Anything that requires a lot of batteries, a lot of attention, or a lot of bandwidth.

Set your alarm! I allow myself 2 hours of time before the start, which is about average. This gives me enough time to feed my horse (or "fluff her food" if she hasn't eaten everything from the prior evening), eat my breakfast, and get everything organized for the day.

Go to sleep. Sometimes this is really difficult. If you can't sleep (common), lie down, stay quiet, and try not to obsess all night.

About CREW, if you're lucky enough to have them

Although a crew isn't necessary to compete in long-distance rides, sometimes you get lucky and some wonderful person will offer to crew for you.

A crew (which can be one person or several) comes to an event to help the rider get through it. Crew is often family—parents, children, spouses, siblings—but can also be friends or even new acquaintances who are interested in learning more about the sport of endurance. Sometimes your crew members are experienced equestrians; sometimes they've never been near a horse.

If you are clever and plan ahead, it's possible to make a crew of any skill level feel helpful, welcome, and valuable.

The most important thing to remember is this: **BE KIND TO YOUR CREW!**

What, exactly, does a crew do?

The crew can perform a variety of services to help the rider in camp and/or in a vet check.

Depending on the age, strength, and experience of your crew, you might ask them to do any of the following:

- Wave and clap and cheer as you enter the vet check.
- Meet you at the in-gate to help you cool the horse.
- Take your horse through the vet's evaluation.
- Trot-out your horse for the vet check.
- Act as a hitching post while you run to the Porta-Potty.
- Care for your horse during the vet check, providing him with access to food and water.
- Care for *you* during the vet check, handing you food and water.
- Restock the saddle and packs with water, food, etc.
- Perform needed repairs on tack.
- Assess your health/comfort needs. Do you need more fluids? More food? A nap or a Band-Aid or a Benadryl? A clean pair of socks or a dry jacket or a warmer sweater or more sunscreen?
- Keep you informed as to the behavior of your horse; for example, is he eating/drinking/resting/peeing normally?
- Try to anticipate your needs for the next leg of the journey: will you need a raincoat, a cold drink, a flashlight?
- Keep an eye on the time so that you and your horse are ready to exit on time.
- Provide cheerful company to you and possibly to other tired, cranky, DIMR riders.
- Take photos.
- Wave and clap and cheer as you leave the vet check for the next stretch of trail.
- Meet you at the next checkpoint. Repeat.

Crewing is often a hot (or cold), dusty (or muddy), and thankless task… unless *you* make sure to thank your crew. One of the effects of DIMR is that riders often seem to misplace the basic politeness they learned in kindergarten. Make an effort to be polite. Especially to your crew.

Here is a basic list of things you may want to provide for your crew:

- A folding camp chair.
- A cooler of food/beverages meant for *them*, not for the riders.
- A paperback book. (*This* book would make excellent reading for crew!)
- Sunscreen, a raincoat, or a lightweight fleece blanket (or all three, depending on the weather).
- Disposable camera.
- Map of the ride and trail description page (if available); write your estimated time of arrival for each checkpoint, as well as a few notes about which supplies you think you will need there.
- An introduction to the RM, the timer, and/or a few friendly people who will be working at the vet check.

- If ride management provides a meal to riders, go ahead and purchase meals for your crew members. It's also a kindness to give a present of some sort to your crew if you are able: a little gift from the tack vendor if there is one in camp or an extra ride t-shirt if any are available. You can also stop on the drive home to buy your crew a nice meal to express your thanks.

It's easy for Monk's rider to find her crew at this busy event! Crew shirts are optional, but fun.

Here's some advice for crew:

DO ask the rider to spend time the day before the ride to list what she would like you to do on ride day.
DON'T ask the rider to make a list of stuff 5 minutes before the start line.

DO take photos of the horse and rider.
DON'T post Facebook photos of the rider covered in electrolyte-and-mud war paint.

DO hand the rider a sandwich.
DON'T hand the rider a sandwich, a can of V8, two bottles of water, clean socks, and a flashlight while she's still holding onto the horse's lead rope.

DO offer to dump a bottle of water on the rider's head in hot weather.
DON'T dump liquid on a rider before she's had a chance to pee.

DO try to anticipate the rider's needs.
DON'T worry if mindreading is outside your skill set.

DO speak clearly.
DON'T holler or cuss.

DO offer to give the horse electrolytes when the rider is getting ready to leave the vet check.
DON'T give electrolytes without checking with the rider first.

DO offer help to a crewless rider when your rider is still out on the trail.
DON'T give away all your rider's food and warm horse blanket if your rider is going to need that stuff later!

DO ask for help from other non-busy crews if you need it.
DON'T flip out if your normally polite rider is so focused on her ride and her horse that she forgets to smile and say "thank you."

DO your best.
DON'T worry about not knowing everything!

DO Take care of yourself, too. If the heat bothers you, find some shade (or make some shade using a horse blanket and the vet's truck). If you are prone to sunburn, wear a hat and use sunscreen. If you chill easily, pack a thermos of hot coffee or tea to drink while you wait for your rider.

DO chat with ride management, other crew, and volunteers. They are very nice people!

DO have fun!

Song "At Mile 94" (with apologies to Sir Paul McCartney)

(to the tune of "When I'm 64")

When I get tired, starting to stare
Many miles from now
Will you still be listening when I start to whine?
Mend my bridle with baling twine?

If I stay out 'till quarter to three
A hundred miles (or more)
Will you still lead me
Will you still feed me
At mile ninety-four?

(Ooooooh) You'll be tired too
And if you say the word
I might crew for you!

I could be handy driving the rig
When you start to yawn
You can mend my breeches by the fireside
Early mornings, go for a ride
Trotting my horse out, while I go pee—
Who could ask for more?
Will you still lead me
Will you still feed me
At mile ninety-four?

Every summer we can go to ridecamp
At Trout Lake or Nile, if it's not too dear
We shall scrimp and save
(Oooooh) Bandages on my knee
Ice pack, vet wrap, tape!

Send me a postcard, drop me a line
Stating point of view
Indicate precisely what you mean to say
Yours sincerely, trotting away.
Here is my entry—fill out the form,
Mine forever more.
Will you still lead me
Will you still feed me
At mile ninety-four?

The Bad Idea Fairy's ridecamp diary part 1

Friday, 2:00 p.m. *Finally I'm ready to pack the trailer and load Hops and go to our first endurance race! I thought that nail artist was going to take all night, but I couldn't imagine going to such an important event without getting my fingernails painted in our special colors—PINK and GREEN forever!*

Friday, 3:30 p.m. *No more room in the trailer. I tried to decide between bringing the PINK fleece cooler or the GREEN fleece cooler, and finally decided to bring them both. Same with the saddle pads. So excited.*

I hope ride management will give me some hay; there wasn't room to pack any in the trailer with all my special gear. I bought a brand-new, pink and green saddle on eBay, and it arrived today, hooray! Just in time for me to pack it for the ride.

Friday, 5:30 p.m. *Getting dark. I guess I'd better load Hops. He's my Sweetie-Oogy-Poo-Bear, and I just wuvs him so much! I hope he gets right into the trailer so we can go.... He hasn't been in it for 2 years, but I'm sure he'll be fine. Despite what happened last time.*

Friday, 6:30 p.m. *He's almost in! I'll give him another pound of sweet feed to encourage him. He has two whorls on his face: that means that he needs lots of encouragement to reach his potential.*

Friday, midnight. *I thought endurance people were supposed to be nice to newcomers. Everybody here was really grouchy when we came into camp. Even the ride manager was a grump when I knocked on her rig door. I have to wait until morning to do my vet check—don't they understand that the ride starts at 6 a.m.?*

They sure aren't very organized around here.

Endurance is a sport that can include the whole family. Here: the Blakely family at the start line of a 50-mile ride.

CHAPTER 11
THE FIRST RIDE, PART TWO

O. M. G. It's finally ride day. What to do first? And…then what?

This chapter is a gigantic timetable of what-happens-when on ride day, plus tips on navigating and staying comfortable on the trail. There is also detailed information about vet checks. Read this chapter before you go to the ride, so you will be ready.

Wake up, greet the day

Set the alarm for 1-2 hours before start time. Get up promptly (no falling back asleep); dress in ride clothes (if you didn't sleep in them), and pull warmer layers over the top, if needed.

Put on sunscreen even if you wake in the dark, so it's already in place when you're on the trail.

Feed your horse and yourself

Ride vets recommend not feeding a large grain meal the morning of a ride. Beet pulp and hay are fine. Check the water bucket too; fill it if necessary.

If your tummy is iffy (common even among experienced riders), try to eat some yogurt or a banana. (See other breakfast food suggestions in Chapter 9). Stash a snack in your pockets to eat on the trail if you get hungry before the vet check.

Tack up, warm up

Your horse may be excited because of all the other excited horses in camp.

Or, your horse may be really, REALLY excited.

Be ready for equine exuberance and allow extra time to cope with it. I like a long warm up on ride morning to focus my mare's attention on me as well as to allow time to get her muscles (and mine) moving. Other riders prefer to start the ride slowly and warm up on the trail without wasting energy before the start of the ride.

Warm up your horse (and yourself) by walking and jogging around the area behind the start line.

If ride management is collecting numbers at the start line, show up *before* start time and give your number. Then continue with your warm up.

The start!

Allow the fast-moving, experienced horses to leave camp first.

Yes, really.

There's nothing more unnerving for an inexperienced horse than to start down a trail only to be bulldozed by a horse and rider aiming to finish first. Sometimes it is difficult to watch others get a head start, but it will make your ride much easier if you aren't in the center of the maelstrom for the first five miles. It's okay to wait 5, 10, or even 15 minutes after the official start time before you hit the trail.

Your horse may be significantly more *FORWARD* than usual, thanks to the excitement of camp and the other horses. Be ready. You may need to school him on the trail, or even put a stronger than usual bit in his mouth for the first few miles. Do whatever you need to do to keep control and stay safe.

The start of a ride can be very exciting to some horses. Start "behind the pack" if you like — and do whatever it takes to stay safe.

Move down the trail—The first leg of the ride

As soon as you are able, pick up your all-day trot and try to stay with this pace as much as possible during the ride.

If you are asked to yield the trail, please do so as promptly as you are safely able; if you wish to pass, ask politely and wait for riders to find a safe place to allow you to pass.

A horse with a red-ribboned tail is a KICKER. Stay back. Call out to the rider so she knows that you and your horse are there.

A horse with a green-ribboned tail is NEW to the sport. Approach carefully and kindly.

A horse with a yellow-ribboned tail is a STALLION. Mare owners, please be courteous.

A horse with a purple/red/green-ribboned tail is visiting from New Orleans. Sing a verse of "When the Saints Go Marching In" as you pass.

At water stops and other places of pause, if other horses are drinking from a water tank when you approach, stay back until they finish and move away. If horses approach the tank as your horse is drinking, allow him to finish, and then ask politely if the other horses will be bothered if you leave. Sometimes horses get so interested in the departure of another horse that they will forget to drink. If your horse is drinking well on the trail, you may wish to administer a dose of electrolytes at water stops.

If you stop along the trail to adjust tack or take a sanitary break in the bushes, expect people to ask if everything is all right. It's okay to say yes. If you actually need or want help, say so. Most folks are happy to assist. If you see someone stopped along the trail, ask after their welfare. It's the polite thing to do.

A rump rug tied behind the saddle can be deployed to keep your horse's "engine" warm at a chilly vet check.

Keeping warm, staying cool (rump rugs, water bottles, & sponges)

If the temperature is cool (i.e., if riders are wearing coats and gloves), provide your horse with a rump rug for the warm up and first few miles of trail. A rug can be wool or fleece and should be rigged to be easily deployed or retracted from the saddle using elastic or strings. When the weather warms and your horse is moving well (about the time you remove your gloves), pull the rug off your horse's bum and tie it securely to the saddle, where it will be handy to re-deploy at the vet check while he's standing still if temperatures are chilly or the wind is blowing. This will help keep warm muscles from growing cold and stiff.

During a 50-mile ride in ambient temperatures, the average horse will burn enough calories to melt a 150-pound block of ice and *then bring that water to a boil.* Remember that the hotter your horse gets, the more he will perspire, which draws water from his blood. This process will measurably thicken the blood, forcing the horse's heart to work harder, beating faster to move the thicker blood.

Drinking water helps replenish fluids, but you can ease the stress on your horse's heart while you're moving by applying cool water to his neck and shoulders. My mare is large-bodied, heavy-muscled, and dark-skinned—a big challenge for cooling. For her, I carry a bottle or two of water designated as squirt bottles that I refill at water tanks, creeks, and puddles to keep a steady supply available. (The bottles are marked with duct tape so that I don't accidently drink swamp water instead of potable water).

When sponging from a creek, be sure to toss the sponge downstream from the horse.

I also carry a sponge on a string: the string is looped around my wrist, and I can drop the sponge from the saddle into a puddle and then squeeze puddle water onto my horse *at a canter*. Practice at home before trying it in competition: the first deployment of the sponge on a string can be very exciting. If sponging from a creek, throw your sponge *downstream* so that the string doesn't wind around your horse's legs.

How to read the markers and navigate an endurance trail

The basic rule of navigating an endurance trail is to keep the trail markers *on your right.*

The ride manager is not obligated to follow this convention, but if the trail-marking system is unusual, the RM will certainly discuss it at the ride meeting — make sure you are there, and take good notes!

At the ride meeting, you will be told what color to follow on the trail. Pay close attention. When trails crisscross or run together, you may see as many as 8 or even 12 differently colored ribbons hanging on a tree branch or fence post. To avoid going off the designated trail for your event, keep track of the color you need to follow. When I'm riding a long event with many loops, I write the loop colors on my arm with a sharpie marker. I've been known to lose the map and the information sheet along the trail, but so far I haven't lost an arm.

Trail markers are commonly made from long strips of surveyors' tape tied or attached with clothes pins to branches, fence posts, or even posts pounded into the ground by the trail crew. The ribbons are hung on the right side of the trail; if you see ribbons only on the left side of the trail, you are going the wrong direction.

Three ribbons mark a turn. (This is a common trail-marking convention but it is not universal.) As you approach a turn, you will see a trio of ribbons instead of a single pair. That means "slow the heck down and look, because you're going to change direction." Some RMs use a long, wide strip of bright yellow or red CAUTION tape to alert riders when a trail has multiple turns. Whichever system is in place, learn it, and watch for it so that you don't wander off course.

Common trail. Sometimes you will encounter a stretch of trail where riders travel in both directions. These common trails are marked with ribbons on both sides of the trail, so that you will have ribbons on the right side no matter which direction you travel. This can be confusing at first. Slow down when you see common trail ribbons, check your map, and make sure you're heading in the correct direction.

Pie plates: not just for dessert anymore. Pie plates or paper plates are handy trail marking devices commonly used at intersections or confusing points, because important information can be written on them with indelible markers.

Trail marking: this white lime powder will not get eaten by elk.

Clues on the ground. RMs will also put trail markings on the ground itself, using white lime powder, chalk, and spray paint. At one recent event, the RM used pancake mix. These substances can be carried easily on a pack horse and then used to draw arrows or even write brief messages on the hillside beside a trail.

The vet check

As you approach the vet check, slow down, dismount, and loosen your horse's girth a notch. Walk beside your horse into the check.

I offer my horse a few carrots, a granola bar, or a handful of grass as we enter. This is her signal for a break and also brings up her gut sounds, which tend to be quiet (a normally functioning gut sounds like a sloshy washing machine).

Walking in to the vet check beside your horse will lower his heart rate.

When you arrive, an in-timer will ask for your vet card. Your arrival time will be recorded. You have 30 minutes to pulse your horse down. Walk him to the water tank for a drink of water. Ideally, your horse will reach the pulse criterion within a few minutes of your arrival. Sponge or scoop water onto his neck to cool him and bring down his heart rate. Scrape the water off to promote faster cooling. Don't sponge out of the water tank; use the smaller sponge buckets provided for this. As you do this, you will notice that the water being scraped off is hot initially. When the water scraped off his skin is no longer hot, his pulse has probably dropped. Step away from the water tank and ask for a pulse.

When the pulser approaches, move your horse's left front foot slightly forward and ask him to stand still. The pulser uses a stethoscope to listen to your horse's heart for 15 to 60 seconds. When the heart rate reaches the required criterion (usually 60-64 bpm), he is "down." The pulser will relay this information to the timer and get a down time and an out time to write on your card.

Your "out time" is the time you are allowed to leave the vet check and continue down the trail. You may not leave before this time, and you must see the vet first.

If there is a long line for the vet, feed your horse (and yourself!) while you wait.

If there's a line, take some hay with you. Allow your horse to eat as you wait. If you've still got food in your pockets, eat it now. The vet will examine your horse quickly but thoroughly. A more thorough explanation of this exam will be covered later in this chapter.

If you are given a passing grade by the vet, get ready to go back out on the trail.

Make sure your horse eats. You need to eat too.

If you haven't peed yet, do that. If you don't need to pee, you haven't been drinking enough fluids. Stay in the vet check and drink more water until you have to pee.

11.1: DIMR—Distance-Induced Mental Retardation

When I first heard about DIMR, I laughed. I was sure it was a joke. And yet, distance-induced mental retardation is a condition readily observed in endurance riders in competition. With DIMR,

the further you ride, the dumber you get.

And it's not a joke. DIMR is real and is the result of a combination of three factors:

- Fatigue;
- Dehydration; and
- Highway hypnosis.

DIMR is inevitable, given the somewhat monotonous and rhythmic nature of endurance riding, which lulls the body and brain into relaxation and leads to an advanced state of dumbness. Marathon runners and Iditarod mushers report similar symptoms in late stages of their events, as do long-haul truck drivers: their focus is on the route ahead and the need to move down it. At break points in the activity, these individuals (like endurance riders) struggle to concentrate, find it difficult to talk to people who are standing still, and cannot describe recent landmarks.

Fortunately, distance-induced mental retardation is temporary, and the effects can be greatly reduced by addressing the root causes of the condition.

Fatigue. If your horse has been properly conditioned for your event, you are probably also adequately fit as well; however, if you need a reason to exercise more, the threat of DIMR is good motivation. The more physically fit you are, the less fatigue you will experience.

Stress also contributes to fatigue level. If you are worried about a lot of things, you will tire yourself unduly. Try to problem solve and stock up on sleep before ride day, so that you aren't completely stressed-out during the event.

Dehydration. Mental acuity begins to diminish in humans at 1% dehydration. Unfortunately, most people begin to feel thirsty at 2%, and at 2% dehydration, you are already a little dumber! Eeek.

Head off dehydration by starting your day with a pint or two of water, not coffee, tea, or Mountain Dew. Drink your morning cuppa if you must, but don't count it as part of your hydration. If you find it difficult to drink a bunch of water in the morning (I do), eat salty food for lunch and dinner the day before to encourage you to drink fluid in advance.

Some people advocate drinking sports drinks during exercise, which ideally contain a nice balance of electrolytes; however, many commercially available sports drinks also contain sugar and gawd-knows-what-else. If you know that you need electrolyte supplementation, do your homework and choose a beverage that will work for you and not make you sicker. Do not try a new sports drink on the day of an event (ask me how I know).

The best way to fix dehydration is to prevent it. A wise endurance rider told me, "If you don't need to pee desperately by the time you arrive at the vet check, you need to stay there and keep drinking water until you do desperately need to pee." (She threatened me with duct tape to keep me in a check until I could prove that I was rehydrated, but that may have been just a threat. Or, maybe not.)

Savvy endurance riders learn to monitor the color of their own urine as well as the color of their horse's urine. As with the horse, a light color is good, dark is bad. If your urine is dark, drink a pint of fluid immediately.

In hot weather, you may need to drink a cup to a quart of water every hour, so figure out in advance where that water is going to be carried (*on your saddle? on your body?*), and practice drinking it in training to establish good habits in competition.

Highway hypnosis. If you've ever driven from Seattle to Missoula with no memory of Idaho, you've experienced highway hypnosis. Highway hypnosis happens when the monotony of repeated stimulus lulls your brain into a semi-hypnotic state. You'd think that the sound and motion would keep you alert, but it numbs your brain, which is already a little numb from fatigue and dehydration, unless you have actively been combating those issues.

How can you fight off highway hypnosis? Keep your brain busy. Chat with your riding partners if you are riding in a group or sing to your horse if you aren't. When you run out of verses, make up new ones... you'll have plenty of time out there on the trail to find the rhymes you need. Consult your map periodically and compare the landmarks you see around you with the landmarks on the map. Compose haiku, text a message to your friends in camp if there's any signal for your phone, or take photos.

In other words, do whatever it takes to keep your brain alert.

DIMR can last a few hours to a few days, depending on the severity of the condition. If you allow yourself to get really dumb, it will take quite a while for your normal sharpness to return. If you intend to drive home the morning after the ride, do everybody on the road a favor and prevent DIMR when you ride, or bring a designated non-DIMR driver.

Refill water bottles and stock up on any supplies you need for saddle packs and pockets.

You can stay at the vet check longer than your required hold. If your horse needs extra time to eat, take it — but be aware that extra time spent at the vet check is not counted as hold time, and you must still get to the finish line before the cut-off set by the ride.

Before leaving, offer your horse a last drink and administer electrolytes if you use them.

As you leave, verify with the timer that you are authorized to go. After checking once more that you are aimed at the trail with correctly colored ribbons for your distance, off you go!

Some people like to leave a vet check at a walk, others prefer to leave like "their ass is on fire" (Summers, 2012). Do whichever you prefer, as long as you are safe.

If the vet does not "pass" your horse, he is pulled from competition. If the horse has lameness or metabolic issues making him unfit to continue, your ride is done for the day.

If the problem is urgent, the vet will immediately start treatment. *But this rarely happens.*

If the problem is not urgent, ask the vet for more information and advice when there is no line. Talk to the timer or other ride management personnel about what to do next. If you are at an out-check away from camp, you will probably be trailered back to camp by a designated driver.

Some riders prefer to leave the vet check at top speed.

Vet criteria — what the vets are looking for (and why)

In the sport of endurance, the welfare of the horse is paramount. The welfare of the horse is more important that mileage points, rider dignity, and it is w-a-a-a-a-a-y more important than a t-shirt completion prize.

The official motto of the sport, "To Finish is to Win," demonstrates the high priority of horse health. In order to "complete," the horse must pass all of the veterinary checkpoints, including the check at the finish line. A horse and rider team might travel the entire distance of an event and then not pass the final vet check. In these cases, they have not "finished the ride" (received a completion). Finish-line criteria are the same as criteria at other points during the ride: the horse must not only be sound and metabolically stable, he must, in the opinion of the veterinarian, be fit to continue. In other words, the horse must be physically able to leave camp and do another loop. *Even at the finish line.*

Knowing this, endurance competitors work with veterinarians to take the best possible care of their mounts before, during, and after competition. The priority of veterinarians at each ride is to ensure the health and well-being of the horses.

Some riders may view the vets as adversaries to be outwitted and outmaneuvered, but this is counterproductive. Vets are committed to assisting riders in completing their events, *as long as the health of the horse is not endangered.* An examining vet may ask another vet for an opinion; however, the head vet has absolute authority to pull a horse from competition.

The vets are merely human and not omniscient; the vet card is designed to give veterinarians as complete and *objective* a view of the competing horse as possible.

The scorecard used by AERC vets has changed a little over time, but still uses the same basic parameters. The card is formatted to allow a veterinarian to complete it as thoroughly and efficiently as possible.

The veterinary exam is something that all horse owners should consider practicing, even if they never plan to attend an endurance ride. Knowing what normal looks like on your horse allows you to more clearly identify abnormal if it ever occurs.

Pulse is measured by listening to the heart rate using a stethoscope in the "armpit" region behind the left front leg. A pulse higher than the predetermined criterion for the event (usually 60-64 bpm) is cause for concern and will eliminate a horse from competition. A very high heart rate can indicate metabolic or emotional distress, or pain.

The heart's function is to move blood through the body to nourish and cool it. If the horse is overheated, the heart pumps faster to provide additional cooling. You can cool a hot horse by applying water to his skin. Use a sponge, scoop, or bucket to apply water to the horse's neck, chest, and belly. (Practice this at home. Belly water tickles!) Immediately scrape off the water with a scraping blade or the flat of your hand. It may feel HOT. If it does, apply more water and scrape it off again. Repeat until the scraped water feels cool.

Contrary to old wives' tales, dumping cold water on a horse's hind end will not cause the muscles to cramp — but it might surprise him into kicking. To cool those large muscles, apply water with a sponge and scrape it off immediately.

A layer of water can actually form a barrier to cooling, so scrape it off again.

The horse's heart will also work harder (and pump faster) if he is dehydrated, because his blood will be thicker. (The change is comparable to the ease of dumping out a glass of cherry Kool-Aid versus the difficulty of dumping out a bottle of thick ketchup). Offer your horse water as often as possible during the event to keep him hydrated. His heart will have an easier task, and he will be less fatigued as a result. For a coherent explanation of this process, read the article on hydration by Garlinghouse, DVM (for a link see Footnoted Resources). The following criteria can be used to roughly measure level of hydration:

Mucus membrane/capillary refill. Press a finger lightly to the horse's gum just above an upper tooth. Time the return to normal (pink) color. Ideally the delay is 1-2 seconds. A refill time over 2 seconds often means the horse is somewhat dehydrated, as does dry or tacky mucus membranes. The mucus membrane test is also accurate for humans, but is customarily performed only between friends.

Jugular refill. Briefly block the jugular vein with a finger or thumb; a refill time of 2-3 seconds is normal and adequate. A horse with a very low resting heart rate (below 32 bpm) may appear to have a delayed jugular refill time, but actually be fine if this is normal for him.

Skin tenting. Pinch a fold of skin at the point of the shoulder. If the skin does not flatten out rapidly, it may indicate dehydration, although this measurement is also influenced by elasticity of the skin and fat content.

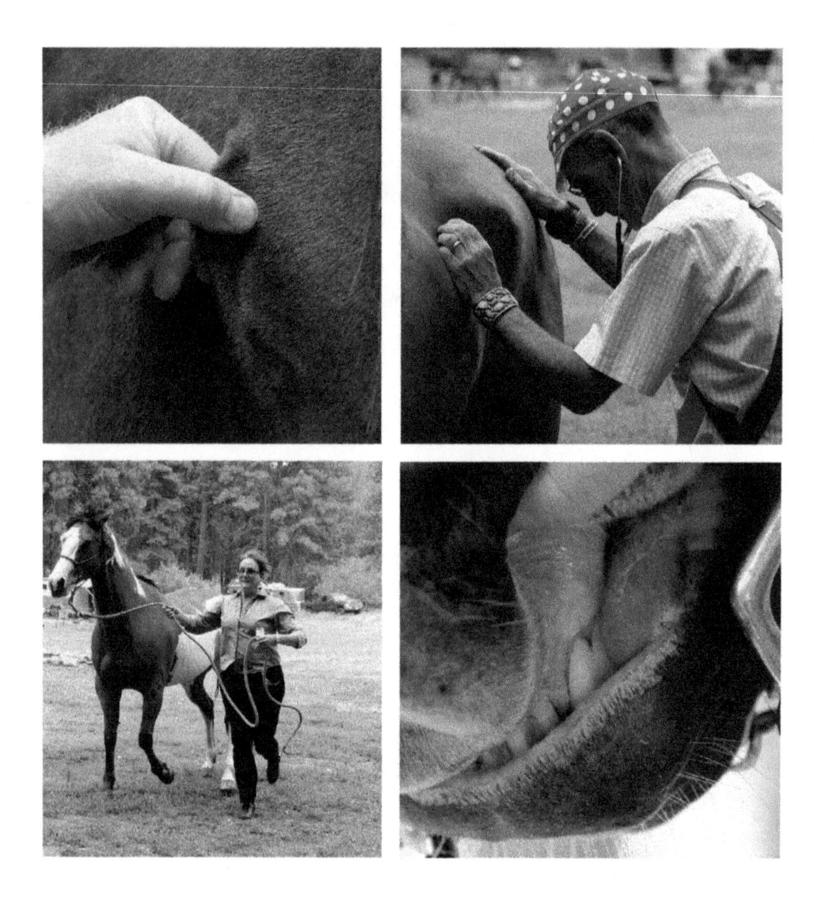

Vets check for hydration, gut sounds, capillary refill, and soundness in motion.

Gut sounds. When a horse is working hard, blood supply is diverted from the gut to the muscles. This is normal; however, prolonged diversion can lead to decreased gut motility or partial and even complete shutdown of the intestines, which are, in layman's terms, Bad Things.

Listen to the four quadrants of the horse's abdomen, two on each side of the barrel, with a stethoscope. A normally functioning gut sounds like a washing machine, with lots of liquid churning noises. Low gut sounds by themselves are not automatically cause for concern; however, if the gut sounds are low and the horse is disinterested in food, water, and his surroundings, it may indicate a stage of colic. Want to know more? Treat yourself to a second article by Susan Garlinghouse: -- "Beating the Metabolic Pull - part II" (link can be found in **Footnoted Resources)**.

Muscle tone. Gently test the firmness of the triceps, butt cheeks, and hams. Don't poke or pinch unless you have significantly better medical coverage than mine. The muscles should feel firm but not hard. Flinching away from this touch indicates muscle soreness or injury.

Anal tone. Lift the tail, evaluating tail muscles and sphincter tone. Firm is good, floppy is not.

The trot-out is usually the final portion of an exam (but not always; sometimes it is performed first). The horse is moved straight out and back at sufficient distance to observe the symmetry and soundness of the gait and the quality of movement. If the horse is an easy-gaited horse, the same parameters of symmetry and soundness are used as the horse moves out at a running walk, tolt, foxtrot, waltz, or electric slide.

The horse may also be asked to trot in a circle each direction, so that consistency of gait can be seen.

Teach your horse to trot-out *before* the event. Chapter 3 has detailed instructions. Practice at home.

Back on the trail

After you've passed the vet check and stayed the required amount of time, return to the trail and pick up your all-day trot again.

When you need to walk on the trail, encourage your horse to stretch his neck down and to each side. This only takes a few strides and will keep him (and you) flexible, even when you become fatigued.

Contrary to the teachings of Pony Clubs everywhere, let your distance horse eat while he's working. A quick snack break every half-hour will keep his guts moving and provide a mental break for both of you. If there is no grass growing along the trail, carry some carrots to feed from the saddle.

As crazy as it seems, you may need to practice this at home so your horse will actually EAT — some get so focused on their work and so excited by the activity of the other horses that they won't eat. It's worth spending the time at home AND at rides to enforce the "eat when I say eat" injunction, so that your horse can refuel between vet checks later in his career when he's doing longer distances. I use the phrase, "*Oh look: food!*" My mare recognizes the words and tone of voice and knows we won't leave again until she's got grass or a carrot in her mouth.

After your snack break, return to your all-day pace.

Sidebar 11.2: The vet card

The examination begins on the left side at the front of a horse, works methodically back to the tail, and then changes to the right side rear, working forward to the mouth of the animal. The parameters are graded A (superior), B (acceptable), C (cause for concern), D (unacceptable and cause for elimination).

You can (and should) practice this exam on your horse at home.

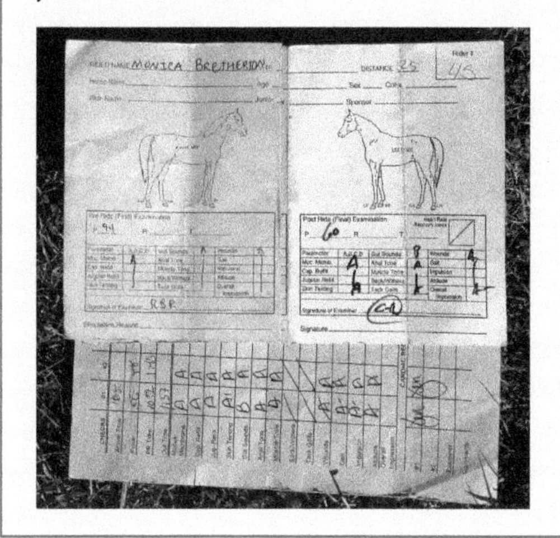

The doldrums

If you hit the doldrums, a point where you, your horse, or both of you start to drag mentally and physically, change what you are doing while still moving down the trail. Ask for a different gait, practice collection or extension, flexion, or lateral movements for a minute or two. Praise your horse's efforts for these exercises. Sing a cheery song out loud. Join up with another rider if you have been riding alone. Or, stay back from the group if you've been riding with others. Set your watch for 5 minutes; walk on a loose rein for that entire time. When your 5 minutes is finished, pick up the all-day trot again.

The Finish Line

When you approach the finish line, SLOW DOWN. Dismount and walk into camp as you did at the vet check.

For LD events, you have not crossed the finish line until your horse has reached the heart rate criterion. Endurance distances (50 miles plus) are considered finished when the horse crosses the line. *All* horses must pass the final vet check in order to complete the event.

As tempting as it is to fly across the finish line, don't. Racing raises your horse's heart rate and level of stress — exactly what you *don't* want at the end of a ride.

When you cross the physical finish line, a finish timer will write the time you arrived on your card. Keep in mind that, for LD events, *your horse has still not crossed the finish line.*

Water is vital for a hard-working horse.

Offer your horse water before beginning your cooling off procedures. If the weather permits, remove your saddle to allow your horse to cool off faster (which brings down his heart rate). In cold, wet, or windy conditions, you may wish to keep the saddle on to keep the horse's muscles warm and loose. Sponge the horse with cool water as you did at the vet check.

When he is cooler, step away from the water tank and ask politely for a pulse. When your horse's heart rate reaches the criterion, the pulser will notify the finish-line timer that he is down.

Your finish time is the time that he officially pulses down.

The final vet check

See the vet for your final evaluation as soon as possible. You have 30 minutes to complete your evaluation after pulsing down in an LD ride, but it is rarely better to allow a horse to stand around before getting the vet check done.

Feed your horse as you wait in the vet line.

If the vet requires "tack off at completion," remove saddle and leg protection if you haven't done so already. If he is wearing hoof boots, they can be left on or taken off, at your discretion.

If the weather is chilly, throw a fleece or wool blanket over him to keep his muscles from getting stiff while waiting in the vet line. If the line is long and the temperatures are low, walk your horse in slow circles as you wait. Honor the place in line of the other riders who are circling their horses.

If the vet has concerns about the soundness or metabolic health of your horse, he may keep your card, advising you to return within 30 minutes after feeding, massaging, or icing the horse.

Follow the vet's instructions. Remember that the vets want you to complete.

Ask for help if you need it.

When the horse passes all parts of the final vet exam, congratulate him and yourself: *You have completed your first distance event!*

Awards

AERC rules state that "all riders who successfully complete the ride must receive a completion award." Sometimes the awards are super neat, like a belt buckle. Sometimes the awards are less costly, like a hoof pick, a bucket, or a t-shirt with the ride logo. Awards are part of the sport, and w you finish your ride, you deserve your award.

Ask ride management when the award meeting will be. Attend! Each finisher is announced individually, so listen for your name. You don't need to make a speech; just hobble to the front of the group and accept your award graciously. It's very nice to thank the ride manager at this point. Then, return to your rig and thank your horse.

The Bad Idea Fairy's ridecamp diary part 2

Saturday morning, 1:45 a.m. *It was sweet of that couple to come out of their tent and set up my metal corral panels for me after I dropped them again. I guess some endurance people are nice. I'll give Hops 15 pounds of grain for dinner so he'll have lots of energy tomorrow, and then I'll drink some whiskey to help me sleep....*

Saturday, 5 a.m. *Wh-a-a-a-a-t??? It's not time to get up yet! Just stay clear of my horse. Don't you understand that he's a STALLION?! I'll get up in just... a little... more... (zzzzzzz)*

Saturday, 6:15 a.m. *Stupid alarm didn't go off! If it weren't for Hops kicking down his corral panels when the other horses left camp, I'd still be asleep. Now I've got to see the vet and tack him up and catch up with everybody on the trail. It's a good thing Purpaloosas really like to gallop.*

Saturday, 7:00 a.m. *That vet is ignorant. He was so busy pretending that Hops was going to bite that he barely admired him at all! Vets are such sissies about stallions. I guess I'll show them when I win this thing. I've seen that movie "Hidalgo" about a million times, so I know all the tricks.*

Saturday, 7:30 a.m. *On the trail at last. We'll gallop and catch everybody! Go like the wind, Hops! We are soo bee-yoootiful with the wind in his mane. Helmets are ugly, don't you agree? And they make my hair all icky. I hope the ride photographer gets lots of pictures of us. Maybe we'll be on the cover of that magazine they have.*

Saturday, 8:15 a.m. *No, Hops, we don't have time to stop at the water tank. We have to go FAST!*

Saturday, 9:30 a.m. *Found the trail again. It's harder to watch for ribbons when I'm texting two people at once. Must remember to text only important people.*

Saturday, 10:30 a.m. *Found the trail again. I must have missed that turn when BFF called with the news about her and Bradsome. So upsetting. It would be okay if he was single, though… cute-o-potamus!*

Saturday, 11:00 a.m. *The vet says that Hops is Grade 2 lame, but he's an idiot. They obviously don't teach vets about the special gates of Purpaloosas. Apparently I don't get 6 hours to finish the ride like everybody else, just because I got started late. Now I only have an hour to get back to camp and win this thing! Quit eating, Hops, we have to race and win now!*

Saturday, 11:50 a.m. Whew! We made it just in time. We didn't finish first because we got lost so much. When I told the manager that the ribbons were confusing, she said the other 54 riders didn't have any trouble. She's really a grump.

Saturday, 12:30 p.m*. What do you mean, because my horse's pulse is still 82 beats per minute I'm disqualified! That's not FAIR! We rode MILES just like everybody else! I WANT A DIFFERENT PULSER! NO, I'M NOT GOING TO STOP YELLING! WHERE'S THAT VET? I WANT TO TALK TO THE MANAGER! I'm not going to take off my pretty saddle here in the DIRT—it's NEW and NICE and your vet check is DIRTY! YOU ARE MEAN! MY HORSE ISN'T AN ARAB SO YOU STUPID PEOPLE DON'T WANT HIM TO WIN!*

BFF just texted me that my hair looks extra-nice when I holler. Passionate. Glad I left that helmet off. It's so important to look good. That should get me what I want, right?

Endurance Bad News

After the ride, some like to nap, some like to chat, some like to graze…or even better: graze cheek-to-cheek!

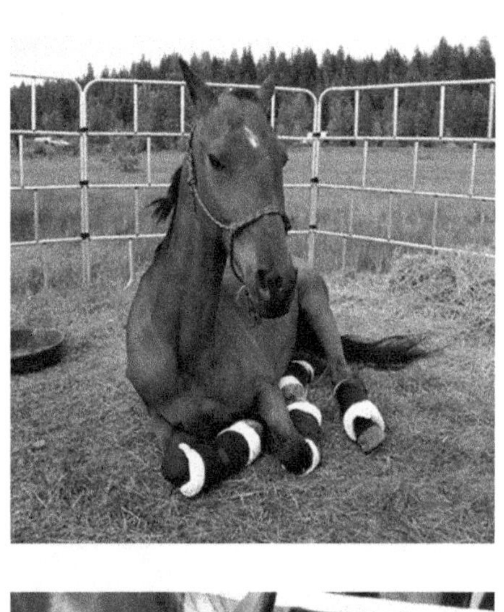

CHAPTER 12
THE FIRST RIDE, PART THREE

Congratulations, you've finished your first endurance event!

Time to kick back with a cold one and socialize a bit with the other riders, right?

Uh, no. Not quite. Your horse worked hard all day, and you took good care of him on the trail. This is no time to quit watching out for him.

When the excitement and adrenaline of the day wears off, your horse may start feeling a little tired and sorry for himself. In most cases, that means he'll sleep well through the night. But not always. Set him up for success by anticipating his needs for the next few days.

This chapter focuses on keeping your equine athlete comfortable during his recovery from the ride and helps you quickly identify any symptoms that might spell trouble. And then, just for fun, a diary entry from the Bad Idea Fairy.

Pulling tack, settling the horse back in camp

After you finish your finish-line vet check, return to your camp and gently take all the gear off your noble steed, carefully looking for scrapes, bumps, swellings, rub marks, or other oddities. If the weather allows, sponge his entire body to remove the sweat crust from his hair and skin. Scrape off the excess water and allow him to dry in the sun if there's sun available. If the weather is cool, cover him with a fleece or wool sheet; if the weather is cold, clean him as thoroughly as you can without chilling those hard-working muscles, and put a blanket on him.

It is not necessary to use liniment, but it won't do any harm. (I love the smell of liniment, don't you?) Avoid applying alcohol-based cleansers to scraped or rubbed hide—it stings! Even if your horse is not normally blanketed at home, an extra layer may provide welcome warmth for fatigued muscles.

Make sure he has plenty of food and water available. It's okay to make his hay "free-choice" at this point, and if he is a fan of beet pulp, go ahead and fill the bucket. Endurance vets recommend that endurance horses refrain from eating a full grain meal before a long-distance ride, but some grain after the event is okay. I take a normal grain meal and divide it into three or four portions for ride day, feeding small portions at vet checks and after the ride.

What to do with the extra poultice? Be creative!

Wait until he's stopped stuffing his face to administer electrolytes. Many horses dislike the taste of electrolytes enough that they will quit eating for a while after a dose. If your horse loves to eat, you can sprinkle some electrolytes into the beet pulp if you've tried this ahead of time and know that he will eat it. (If there is any doubt, wait until he's had plenty of food before giving him a dose.) Keep an eye on the water bucket also: eating hay encourages horses to drink water, and hydration is a condition to be devoutly desired.

What about alfalfa? There is a bit of an argument about alfalfa as a feed for endurance horses, but in general, after a ride I throw a few handfuls on top of the hay pile. I tend to think of alfalfa as a garnish or sauce sprinkled on top, rather than a food, like a plate of spaghetti. If you want to educate yourself about feeding alfalfa to distance horses, read Susan Garlinghouse's article on Alfalfa (link provided in **Footnoted Resources**).

If your horse is picking at his food after a long day of work, by all means offer a flake of alfalfa to re-ignite his appetite. If your horse is a picky eater, or seems disinterested in food after an event, seek out some fresh green grass.

A horse who is not interested in grass may be experiencing early symptoms of colic, so if he turns up his nose at grass or alfalfa (especially if he is the kind of horse who normally loves his food), listen with a stethoscope (or your ear) to his gut sounds. If you don't hear noises that sound like the scrub cycle of a washing machine, it is time to ask for some veterinary advice. Early intervention is the best kind. You will not jeopardize your "finish" by alerting the vet staff to a potential problem, and you might save yourself and your horse a long and painful night.

If he is acting normally, allow your horse some time to eat and snooze. Then, after he's been back in camp for a few hours, take him for a quiet stroll around camp. Make a point of visiting all the water tanks, walking slowly enough for your horse to grab a bite of grass every few strides. Stop and talk as you meander. Ask other people about their day and be ready to talk about yours. It doesn't matter how long it takes you to walk around camp; the important thing is to allow your horse to stretch his legs and unkink his muscles before he settles down for the night.

Poultice? Ice? Walking?

Some folks swear by a mud poultice after a long ride to cool the legs, support the tendons, and reduce "stocking up" (puffiness in the lower legs) after exercise. I have never needed to poultice legs thus far, and I can almost always find a deep spot in cool creek water to stand my horse in, or a hose, or even a deep rubber bucket full of cold water. (My horse is abnormally tolerant of my strange requests, including a request for her to stand with her legs in buckets of water.)

If you would like to apply a poultice and have never done it, ask one of the vets to advise you. The same goes for applying supportive bandages: if you haven't applied leg bandages before, get somebody to teach you to do it properly.

A leisurely walk a few hours after the finish will allow your horse to stretch his legs and snack while you trade ride stories.

Ice boots are a good alternative to a poultice. Ice boots are strapped on like shipping or splint boots, using Velcro. They are generally filled with gel packs designed to be frozen and thawed many times; I buy replacement gel packs cheaply at the marine supply stores near home that serve local sport fishermen.

Some horses like to be fussed over and groomed after a ride; others prefer to be left alone. The gelding I rode for years was a social butterfly and would happily follow me everywhere through camp as I did a million little tasks. My current mare prefers to turn her face to the trailer, cock a hip, and ignore the rest of the world while she naps. Learn what is normal for your horse and try to abide by his preferences whenever possible. You may want to fuss over him and bring him a thousand treats and kisses, but he deserves to be given the treatment he prefers on the evening after a ride.

Night

I make a point of checking on my horse at least twice during the night after a ride. These checks are not formal or extensive; in fact, I sometimes don't even get out of bed. I do shine a flashlight on her to see if she's behaving normally—either eating or sleeping. For *my horse,* these are normal behaviors after a ride. If you have never checked on your horse during the night, you may not know what is normal, but generally speaking, eating and sleeping are good things. Bad things include, but are not limited to, moaning, shifting weight from foot to foot, looking anxious, kicking at the flanks, excessive and repeated rolling, and an absence of recent manure. If I saw any of the last three items on that list, I would run-not-walk for the vet.

Afraid you are going to sleep through a night alarm? Drink a quart of water before bedtime. If you are like me, your bladder's clock will wake you before 2:00 a.m.

Après ride routine—the next few days

The morning after the ride is a repeat of the evening routine. Supply plenty of food and water, run your hands over your horse's body and note any tenderness or swelling, pay attention to his interest in the activities around you. Take him for a walk to loosen up his muscles. After he's finished his breakfast, a dose of electrolytes will help him maintain hydration during the trailer ride home.

Break up your camp and get everything ready for loading your horse. Take one more walk around camp with your horse and stop at the water tank to give him an opportunity to drink before you leave. Then, load him up and head on home!

If your drive is more than 4 hours long, try to stop every 2-3 hours to give your horse a break (these rest breaks can be refueling and potty breaks for you as well). It is not necessary to let him out of the trailer, but he will appreciate the cessation of motion for a few minutes. Offer water or a few bites of sloppy beet pulp or a handful of carrots and apples. My horses travel with hay bags in the trailer, so they often "eat their way home" from an event, arriving just a little fatter than when they left.

For the next 3 or 4 days, keep a closer than usual eye on your faithful steed. Make sure he continues to eat and drink normally. You may want to continue providing electrolytes for a day or two after returning home to encourage your horse to drink plenty of water.

Monitor his enthusiasm about being turned loose in the pasture and compare his post-ride and normal behavior. He may seem a little quieter for a few days, or he may seem especially bossy when he is turned out with his usual herd. With experience, you will learn how quickly your horse bounces back from an event. If you see anything odd, call your vet and explain what you see.

After a few days, work him lightly, beginning with a short arena session or a hand walk down the road. After a difficult 50 miler, I usually wait a week or longer to return to our normal trail-riding routine; the time off after a shorter event can be less, depending on the experience level and fitness of the horse.

When I see my horse trotting around the pasture and chasing the goats as she did before we left for camp, I know it's time to go back to work.

The Bad Idea Fairy's ridecamp diary part 3

Sunday, 1:00 p.m. *Well, that ride manager certainly knows how to treat people if they stick up for their rights, but I'm still outta here. All I got for all this work is a stupid t-shirt, no points or anything… meh, it isn't even pink and green so it's not like it'll go with any of my outfits.*

The vet doesn't want me to leave camp yet because Hops' heart rate is still higher than 70. But, whatever; I've got to get back home and get my nails re-done. These people don't deserve to have a great horse like Hops around here.

I'm sick of endurance and these stuck-up people.

I think I'll do reining with Hops instead. I saw a pink and green western saddle on eBay that will look really cute on him!

For Sale - tack included
(you catch & load)

If you are pulled from the ride at an out-check, you will be trailered back to camp by volunteers.

CHAPTER 13
WHEN THINGS GO WRONG

Things go wrong at rides all the time. Sometimes the glitch is minor, like a forgotten water bottle or a loose shoe. Sometimes things go wrong in a much bigger way.

This chapter prepares you for all kinds of pear-shaped activities, with the hope that all of your mishaps will be minor.

I wonder if Mark Knopfler, lead singer for the band Dire Straits, ever rode endurance, because the song "The Bug" (look it up online) completely captures the experience of the sport.

If you ride enough miles, "a rock with your name on it" will eventually throw itself into your path. If not a rock, a hole. Perhaps your horse will be a little off at a vet check—not near death, certainly, but not qualified to continue the ride—then be perfectly sound a few days or even hours later.

As riders, and especially as endurance riders, we need to accept that some horses are gigantic suicidal machines. Horses can and do injure themselves in the strangest, most bizarre and ill-timed ways imaginable. If you are lucky, your horse will find his rock at home in the pasture during your off-season, and you need only pet his nose and say "poor baby" for a day or two until he is sound again.

But what if something happens at a ride?

Lameness pulls

The most common reason that a horse is disqualified (or pulled) from a ride is lameness. There are 5 degrees of lameness, described as follows:

- Grade I. Difficult to observe and not consistently apparent. This is the horse with an intermittent bobble to his gait.
- Grade II. Difficult to observe at a walk or trotting a straight line; consistently apparent under certain circumstances, such as working in a circle. This horse shows himself to be lame inconsistently, since you don't ride down the trail in 20-meter circles.
- Grade III. Lameness consistently observable at a trot under all circumstances.

- Grade IV. Obvious lameness at a walk: marked nodding, hitching, or shortened stride.
- Grade V. Minimal weight-bearing in motion and/or at rest; inability to move.

AERC rules require that a horse that is consistently lame be pulled from competition, even if the lameness is very slight. Therefore, a horse that is Grade III, IV, or V lame must be pulled.

It seems crazy sometimes, but a horse that takes a huge lame step every 11th stride can be cleared to continue, but a horse that is showing a tiny bit of left front-foot soreness must be pulled.

This is where a helpful vet and canny rider can put their heads together to make decisions to benefit the horse. A rider can ask for 30 minutes to try to bring the horse back to soundness. If the horse's lameness is caused by a stone in the shoe, a tight groin muscle, or even an abscess in the hoof, it is sometimes possible to resolve the problem in the time allowed, return to the vet check to get the vet's approval, and then go on and finish the ride.

Ride vets can help prevent a small problem from becoming a bigger problem. In this case, the loan of a saddle pad saved the day.

Sometimes a rider and vet must try to determine if the lameness is caused by something that will get better or worse if the horse continues to compete. In some cases, as with an arthritic mare I used to ride, exercise can improve the horse's comfort and way of going. In other cases, as with a gluteal muscle pull experienced by a seasoned gelding I rode for many years, even moderate movement can make pain substantially worse. Although both of my horses presented with Grade II lameness, it was better to allow the mare to compete and better to pull the gelding for the day.

So what should you do when you see the vet shaking her head?

- ***Don't panic.*** Lameness is rarely fatal. You might be pulled from the day's competition, but it's entirely possible that your horse will be sound again in time to compete at the next ride.
- ***Try not to cry.*** This is easier said than done, especially if you are a little tired, a little dehydrated, and more than a little worried about the well-being of your horse.
- Without arguing or holding up the line if other horses are waiting, ***ask for more information*** about the lameness. Does it appear to be a foot problem, a leg problem, a hip or shoulder issue? Could his back be sore because of an ill-fitting saddle?

It's okay to ask someone else to trot-out your horse for you, so that you can observe the lameness in action. Be polite and kind. Remember that the vet may not have gotten enough sleep the night before, but she is there to help not hinder you.

One of the best questions you can ask a vet is, "What would you do if this was your horse?"If the vet observes a Grade I or Grade II lameness, she may offer suggestions or advice for you. LISTEN TO THE VET'S ADVICE. If it's a tight muscle causing the problem, some warm towels and a massage may fix it. Foot soreness may be helped by adding a hoof boot or by removing the existing boot and washing the sand out.

Remember that AERC has a very strict no-drug policy, so if your horse requires a dose of bute or even herbal remedies such as arnica or devil's claw to feel better, he is done for the day. The complete list of prohibited substances can be found in the AERC Member's Handbook.

If you are pulled from competition, make arrangements with the vet to re-examine your horse later, when there are no other teams waiting in line. This gives the vet a chance for a more complete examination, so that she can give you more specific instructions and you can make better decisions about how to treat the horse for the best chance of recovery.

Care for your entire horse, not just the lame part. Don't forget that he still needs food, water, a warm blanket if the weather is cold, and possibly some electrolytes to aid in his recovery from exercise.

Metabolic pulls

A horse may also be pulled from competition for metabolic issues.

If a horse fails to meet the ride criterion (pulse recovery), or if he has "thumps" (synchronous diaphragmatic flutter, a warning sign of serious fluid and electrolyte imbalance), he will be pulled from competition.

Likewise, he can be pulled if he exhibits signs or symptoms of metabolic distress, such as extremely low gut sounds, dehydration, an elevated CRI, or notable loss of appetite or attention. One of these symptoms by itself does not mean that your horse will automatically be pulled, but two or more symptoms are cause for concern. The purpose of having qualified veterinarians as judges at endurance rides is to ensure that a horse will be pulled from competition before it is overtly sick and in need of treatment.

Horses that are metabolically distressed at or after a ride may require treatment, such as intravenous fluids, or may even need to be transported to a veterinary hospital. Such treatment is not included in your ride fee and must be negotiated with the attending vet.

This is how you want your ride to be...but sometimes it doesn't happen that way.

Rider-option lameness, rider-option metabolic, ADR

You find yourself in a situation where your horse passes all of the veterinary criteria, but you feel or see that something is wrong. Vets call this ADR, or "Ain't Doin' Right." The vet staff sees your horse for only a few minutes out of every few hours during competition, but you are with your horse all day long; ultimately, the welfare of the horse is your responsibility.

If you think there is something wrong with your horse, you are probably right, and AERC has created statistic pull codes for situations like this. If your horse passes the vet check, but you decide that something is wrong, you can take a "rider-option" pull.

Remember, nothing further down the endurance trail will make your horse less tired, less hungry, or less sore.

If you feel your horse is not *sound* enough to continue, even if the vet has judged him Grade I or Grade II, he will be coded RO-L (Rider-option, Lame). If you decide that something *metabolically* "ain't right" with your horse, the pull code will be listed as RO-M (Rider-option, Metabolic).

13.1: Peeing Pink

I attended a ride recently with a very fit mare. She finished 25 miles with excellent vet scores, and was hungry and clearly mentally ready to go out and do another 25 miles. However, while standing and resting at the vet check, my mare peed urine the color of strawberry lemonade. I recognized this as a very early symptom of tying up (Exertional Rhabdomyolisis), and quickly ran back to the vet to surrender my card and withdraw from the ride.

In a later vet exam, my mare showed no other symptom of tie-up. She was eating, drinking, peeing, pooping, and moving freely as usual. However, discolored urine indicates a metabolic problem that will not improve with more exertion, and in fact can cause permanent injury. Thankfully, my mare recovered fully from her incident and has gone on to compete successfully again.

Learn from my example: when in doubt, take extra time at the vet check and don't be afraid to ask for a rider-option pull from the event.

This is not a "newbie only" circumstance, and nothing to be ashamed of, if or when it happens to you. Endurance riders are very proud of their "welfare of the horse" ethic, and will praise you for taking good care of your steed.

Rider-option pulls

There is one other pull code, which relates to the *rider* and not the horse. If a pull is listed in the finishing stats as RO, it is because the rider (not the horse) was too sick or injured to continue the ride. There is a tongue-in-cheek code which riders sometimes threaten to use: RO-AHF, which translates as "Rider Option, Ain't Having Fun." Hopefully, you will never want to use that code!

If you pull from competition at an out-vet check (away from the main ridecamp) you will be trailered back to camp by a designated driver. If trailer space is limited and another horse or rider is in more distress than you and your horse, offer to let them go first. If your horse doesn't need your attention while he's waiting for the ambulance ride back, tie him somewhere with access to food and water and lend a hand getting other riders through the vet check—this help is appreciated and may distract you from dwelling on your misfortune.

Getting pulled is often emotionally difficult, and yet it is a real and important part of a sport that places the welfare of the horse above the ego of the rider. Deciding to pull your own horse is sometimes even more difficult, as riders tend to second-guess themselves after the event. However, heeding those gut feelings rarely leads to a bad decision.

You'll remember that the endurance rider's motto is "To Finish is to Win"; an alternate motto might be "Pull Today and Ride Another Day."

Or maybe, if Mark Knopfler of Dire Straits is right, you just need to wait for the day when you are the windshield and not the bug.

Getting lost, getting found again

If you are trotting down the trail and cannot see a ribbon and realize you cannot remember the last time you saw a ribbon, you may be off route.

Before you panic, look at the ground. Do you see a lot of hoof prints in front of you, travelling in the same direction? Do you see fresh manure on the trail? Those are signs that riders from your event have been here and you really *are* on the right trail. Also, look carefully at the ground below the place where you think a ribbon marker should be.... Maybe you can spot a ribbon tossed there by the wind.

If you're still not convinced you're in the right place, look up. You may not see ribbons hanging from branches, but can you spot a clothespin or stub of ribbon? Hungry cattle can't reach as high as deer or elk, so they "spaghetti" the ribbons that they can reach, and then stop sucking in when they get to the clothespin, leaving orphaned clothespins high overhead on tree branches. If you can see those clothespins, you're probably in the right place. You may also be able to see that the trail has been trimmed back by trail crews with loppers. If you see recently trimmed branches at eye-level for a rider on horseback, you are probably not really off trail.

It could just be trash along the trail, except for the tell-tale clothespins.

But what if you ARE off trail? A few words of advice:

- ***Don't panic.*** Before you go any further, stop, take a drink of water, and breathe. Check your trail map or your GPS, if you carry one, and try to figure out where you are. Think back to the last time you saw a trail marker.
- ***Mark your location.*** Tear up a bandana and tie a strip of cloth to a tree branch, stick a scrap of paper under a rock in the middle of the trail, make a pile of rocks or branches on the right side of your trail to mark where you are now, or partially break off a branch beside the trail and leave it dangling. This gives you a landmark that you can return to if you can't find the trail. You do not want to get more lost.
- ***Look in all directions for clues to the trail.*** Remember that your trail is marked for riders; stay on your horse so you can see markers that are 6-8 feet off the ground.
- *Backtrack, if possible.* If you aren't sure you're going in the right direction, mark the trail as you go with strips of cloth tied to branches, piles of rocks, or dangling branches. Scuff an arrow into the dirt with your boot to indicate the direction you travel.
- *Listen for other riders.* They may not be talking, but you may hear hoof beats or tack jingling.
- ***Stay with your horse.*** If he is without the company of horses for a long time and then hears other horses, he will holler.

If you are separated from your horse

Sometimes a horse will get spooked and take a notion to hare off—either from the trail or from camp—into the hinterlands, leaving you behind. Years ago, a horse I took to a ride in Prineville, Oregon, got scared in the middle of the night, blew through his electric pen, and was lost for 4 days.

This horse, whom we called The Toad (for good reason), took his gelding buddy with him when he ran, so we couldn't use his buddy as bait to lure him home. However, if you lose a horse but NOT your horse's best friend, take the buddy with you when you search. With luck, the buddy horse will holler and your horse will come a-running.

Know your horse! We wasted valuable time searching the creek bottoms and canyon floors for our missing horses, because knowledgeable people told us that horses are lazy and will head downhill instead of uphill. Our horses were Arab geldings fit for 50-mile rides. They ran uphill. Know your horse, act accordingly.

If your horse is food motivated, take a shaker can with you—either with grain in it or something that sounds like grain—that you cobble together from stuff you can find quickly. If you normally summon your horse with a whistle or a distinctive shout, teach other searchers to copy your call.

The Toad was a distinctively marked bay gelding with a ride number written on his bum when he left camp; I could describe him easily to other searchers. If your horse is a plain brown or grey wrapper, add some kind of identification so that people can tell that the horse they've found is yours (see the sidebar in Chapter 9). I use a dog tag engraved with the horse's name and my cell phone number braided into the horse's mane. I attach similar tags to my horse's bridle and saddle, so that if those items are found they will return to me.

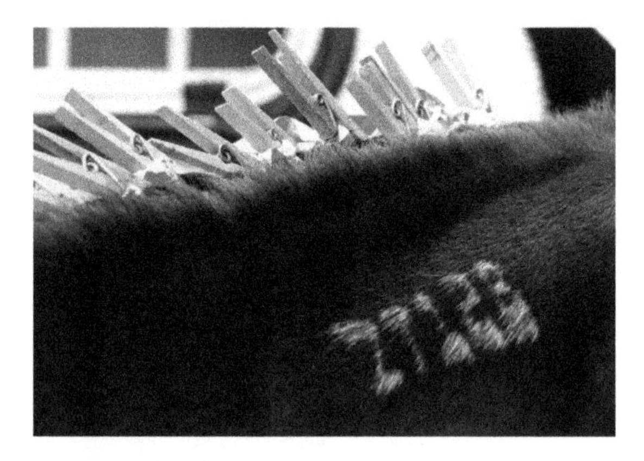

A freeze brand doesn't require any technology to read.

My current horse is a plain brown wrapper, but she is distinguished by her freeze brand, which shows her USTA registration number. If your horse is nondescript, consider having him branded, freeze-marked, or micro-chipped. I take photos of my horse each summer around July 4th and each winter around New Year's, so that I have recent pictures showing conformation and markings with a seasonally appropriate haircoat. I hope I never have to put these photos on a "lost horse" poster, but if I need them, I've got them.

The photos also have ME in them, proof that I had possession when the picture was taken, which a sheriff will appreciate. I have all my horses brand inspected, and the laminated ID cards issued by the state are kept in a secure location in the horse trailer.

Who do you call if your horse is lost? Here's a starter list:

- ***Contact everyone within shouting distance***, including neighbors, riding partners, other riders, and people riding bikes, walking dogs, and hiking with kids.
- If your horse is lost in the wilderness, *contact the local chapter(s) of the Back Country Horsemen.* Many of these people will also be members of the local Search and Rescue, if there is one—and if they aren't, they will know how to contact S&R.
- *Call law enforcement,* including city cops and sheriffs. If you're near a state road or highway, call the state police also. If you're in a park, call the rangers.
- *Contact animal control offices.* Ask the cops—some areas have multiple animal control agencies, and you want to talk to them all.
- *Talk to construction crews, loggers, or road and trail crews* if any are working nearby.
- *Visit local auction yards.* If somebody finds your horse and wants to sell him because they haven't seen your posters, you will want the auction staff watching for your horse so he doesn't get sold to a kill buyer.
- *File a report* on NetPosse.com, which operates a nationwide alert system for lost and stolen horses.
- If the horse is in an open area, *consider enlisting a local airplane or helicopter pilot* in the search.
- *TALK TO KIDS.* Kids and teens will often keep looking long after the adults have lost hope and interest.
- You should also make up a simple poster with this information:

LOST HORSE

Breed, gender, color and markings

Last known location of the horse, and date lost

PHOTO

Your contact info (tearaway strips are good)

Make a billion color copies. Post it everywhere. Send it to everyone: gas stations, feed stores, gear shops, grocery stores, back-country riding groups. Send it to the local newspaper. Also send the poster via email to everyone you know.

Then grab your shaker can and put on your sturdiest walking shoes. Get out there and look.

Most of the lost horses I know of are found, usually within a few days.

Sometimes lost horses are gone for a month or more. Keep looking. It's hard, I know. Keep looking anyway.

13.2: Even Monkeys Fall

My 8th-grade English teacher used to say, "even monkeys fall out of trees." I had to think about that phrase for a while before I understood what she meant—that even the most experienced folks can make dumb mistakes.

Pacific Northwest region rider Darlene Anderson has mentored many new riders and started many young endurance horses, but she is the first to admit it when she's made a mistake, like the time she got dumped on the trail by a young stallion she was training. After the incident, she left the following post on her Facebook page:

5 things I did right

1. Told someone where I was, when I left, and when I expected to be back.

2. Used my safety gear. I had my crash vest and helmet on. The crash vest prevented injury, I know it. Injury may have only involved a few bruises, but if they looked anything like what's on my bum, then I'm glad I don't have 'em! I also had a halter & leadrope on my horse. My saddle was secure with properly fitted breast collar and crupper. I didn't worry too much I'd find him w/the saddle under his belly.

3. Stayed on the trail after losing track of my horse. Lots of people get themselves in more trouble when they stray off the path and get themselves lost.

4. Wore sensible shoes. I had the privilege of walking about 10 miles yesterday. I was thankful for the running shoes I had on. I was thinking to myself... I had LOTS of time to think in the 2 hours it took me to get home, that I was glad I didn't have any bulky shoes on my feet. It was 80 degrees out. Would not have been fun.

5. Called for reinforcements as soon as I figured out I wasn't going to find the horse in that huge area alone.

Mistakes I made

1. Stored my phone in my pommel bag instead of on my person. My phone took a walkabout with the horse and that big dummy doesn't know how to get it out of the bag to answer it! If I had had my phone on ME, I could have called for help finding my horse much sooner than the 2 hours it took me to hike home.

2. Riding alone when home alone.

3. Not having any information about me on my person. My crash vest has this little pocket w/a card in it that has room for info about me. Who I am, my blood type, emergency contact. Have I ever filled that out? Heck no.

Now on my list of things to do/get

1. Some sort of leg holster for my cell phone.

2. Place an info card with pertinent info in the holster w/the phone.

3. Fill out info card in my crash vest.

4. Make sure everyone who helped is properly thanked.

Junior Nikki Knisley and her sponsor Andie Holstrom enjoy a great day at the 2010 Milwaukee Road Rail Trail ride.

CHAPTER 14
JUNIOR RIDERS

Junior riders are my all-time favorite riding companions. They know all kinds of stories and songs that they will share with me, and when I get tired they are usually just getting warmed up. I can't think of another physical endeavor that throws unrelated adults and kids together in such a haphazard—and yet, nurturing—manner. It turns out that, when people spend time together in the wilderness, working towards the common goal of getting healthy horses to the finish line, they take care of each other, even when one of the people is young and the other is not so young.

This chapter focuses on the special circumstances relating to Junior riders: the AERC rules, the bright side(s) to being a Junior, and the process of emancipation for qualified Juniors. It includes advice for adults who are parenting Junior riders, and some tips for finding good sponsors. We finish with a song you can sing in back in camp.

AERC rules and regulations for Juniors

The AERC Rules and Regulations book has an entire section devoted to the special needs of and requirements for Junior riders.

14.1: AERC Rules

- Junior riders in both full and LD rides, whether AERC members or not, must be accompanied by a competent adult (21 years or older) sponsor throughout the competition.
- Juniors are riders who are less than 16 years old on December 1st.
- Juniors must wear a helmet.
- Juniors may change sponsors only at vet checks. Sponsorship may change between checks only in the event that a competitor or a competitor's mount is unable to continue forward safely.

The rule about sponsors is listed first because it is the most important and is non-negotiable: Juniors must ride with an adult.

What the rule doesn't say is that competent Juniors often sponsor their adult companion(s), especially on longer rides. While Junior riders are younger and thus more vulnerable and sometimes need guidance, senior riders are older and thus more fragile and sometimes need youthful assistance! It's lovely when you drop your water bottle at the 48-mile mark of a 50-mile ride, and before you can heave a heavy sigh, the Junior beside you is on the ground, handing it back up!

If adult riders are lucky, they'll get to sponsor awesome experienced juniors.

Who is a Junior?

Just as Thoroughbreds celebrate their official birthday on January 1st, regardless of actual foaling date, a Junior's age is calculated as of December 1st, the first day of the national ride season.

The Helmet Rule

Helmets are required for Junior riders; however, I encourage my Juniors to encourage their other sponsors to wear a helmet as well. If Juniors are smart, they ask (sweetly and kindly, of course) if the sponsor already owns a helmet, or if they would prefer that the Junior go find one for the sponsor to borrow.

Changing sponsors

I have lost track of the number of times I have come into a vet check and had ride management give me *that look,* signifying that they have a sponsor-less Junior for me to take forward.

14.2: Advice to a new rider riding with an experienced Junior

An adult friend of mine wanted to ride a novice event on an experienced mare, but she was nervous about getting lost and generally finding her way through the endurance process. We located an experienced Junior and told my friend, "This is Meagan, the Junior you will be sponsoring. Do everything the Meagan tells you to do and you will be fine."

And they were.

Kids take such good care of their horses, that it is often not the *Junior's* horse that gets stuck. Instead, it's almost always the sponsor or the sponsor's horse that needs a lift back to camp. In circumstances like this, it is entirely okay for the Junior to continue forward with another competent adult.

Savvy endurance kids know that stuff happens on the trail, and they line up a bunch of potential sponsors in advance. Still, "stuff happening" can occasionally include all potential sponsors being pulled. This happened to my young friend Jill. Her horse was still good to go, but a number of her sponsors (including me) had gotten pulled during the course of the day for a variety of reasons. When it came to the last leg of the ride, Jill was in last place, and there were no more competitors left in the ride to go with her. Undeterred, the ride manager turned to me. "If you can ride another 13 miles, I'll loan you my horse," she offered. I grabbed my helmet, hopped up on the borrowed horse, and Jill and I did the last leg together so that she could get her completion. The rules do allow a last-place Junior to go forward accompanied by an adult running along beside, but I can't imagine doing it myself!

Junior riders are always ready for another loop

The bright side(s) of being a Junior

Junior riders at many rides are eligible for additional prizes. Several of the RMs in my region offer a "Junior BC" prize in any event that has more than three Junior entries. This arrangement provides an extra incentive for Junior riders (and their parents/adult sponsors) to attend those rides. This is a bonus to the ride manager and is also an excellent way for RMs to spotlight the excellent care that Junior riders show for their horses.

Juniors also qualify for discounted ride entries at some rides. If you are a Junior rider and do not see a discount offered, ask.

Emancipation

A rider 14 years or older who has completed 500 AERC miles or more (in any distance combination) may "emancipate" in order to ride without a sponsor.

The emancipation process requires that the Junior and his/her parent write a letter to the AERC office well in advance of an event, requesting and consenting to the unsponsored status. (Note that a ride manager does not have to honor the emancipation, however). Emancipated Juniors ride in the senior division. Juniors can be incredibly savvy and sometimes more competent than their senior rider sponsors. And as outrageous as some adults may find the concept of allowing teens to ride a horse all alone, for many miles, in the wilderness, endurance parents quickly learn that most kids who qualify for emancipation really can handle almost everything that happens on the trail.

In fact, the "parenting" of endurance Juniors is a shared task accepted by many adults in the endurance community. Some kids come to events with family members, but many others come with neighbors, riding instructors, or with interested adults who recognize that a horse kid needs to spend time with horse people and who are willing to move heaven and earth to make sure that this time is offered. Lest you worry that these unparented kids are wont to run wild in camp, let me assure you: kids in a ridecamp have work to do. They know what needs doing, they know who needs to do it, and they make sure it all gets done. If you ever want to meet a bunch of mature, responsible, totally fun kids, please come visit us in ridecamp sometime.

Sponsors—How to find a good one, how to be a good one

It's not always easy for kids to ride off into the wilderness with adults they don't know very well. Sometimes the adults ride too fast for the Junior's horse. Juniors tell me it can be awkward to ask the adult to slow down, and they usually just bide their time until the vet check, where they try to find a slower-moving sponsor. Sometimes the sponsor moves so slowly that the Junior despairs of ever finishing the ride. And sometimes they don't have any option other than to suck it up and cope as best they can.

Sometimes the junior's horse is as entertaining as the kid.

Kids tell me that they really hate riding with adults who complain a lot or married couples who spend the entire ride arguing. The kid network is quick, though—and they tell each other which adults to avoid and which to seek out when a sponsor is needed. I'm honored that they keep coming back to me, and I think that they think I'm nicer than I feel, especially at the end of 50 miles!

Endurance Juniors are smart, cool, and excellent company. They sing the songs they know and tell me stories. On longer rides, older teens sometimes want to confide—something I encourage—with the understanding that I will talk to their folks after the ride. I am honest about this and when talking with kids in general.

14.3: Picking up Juniors

Once, I picked up the grandson of an adult competitor at the first vet check of a 50-mile ride. At the time, I barely knew the grandfather and had seen 10-year-old Chad only once or twice before in my life.

Grandpa Chuck's horse was lame and pulled from competition, and Chad was a little shy of heading off into the wilderness with a strange adult and the handful of teen girls riding with me that day. However, Grandpa Chuck assured me that the kid was "a good hand," and when our horses checked through, we all trotted cheerfully away towards the second vet check… where we were met by Chad's very concerned father, who was acting as crew that day.

When Dad saw the smile on Chad's face, put there by riding his big red gelding on some of the most beautiful mountain trails in the world in the company of five pretty girls (plus me), he threw up his hands and welcomed us all to camp. "If I'd known you were riding with them," I heard him tell his son, "I'd have come along with you!" Chad, a young man of few words, just grinned and grinned and grinned.

When riding with Juniors, keep an eye on what the rider eats and drinks. They will feed only the choicest hay and freshest grass to their ponies, but forget that a pack of Skittles and a can of Mountain Dew is not adequate nutrition for themselves. It's not too difficult to pack extra yogurt and almonds in my vet-check box, so I try to do that if I suspect that I'll be riding with a Junior. Other items I pack for my younger companions include a heavy trash bag (aka emergency raincoat) and a tube of sunscreen. They might tease me about "anointing" them with sunscreen, but they take the lotion, and they put it on without complaint, bless them.

Juniors don't like to be treated like dummies or like second-class citizens, and sometimes it is up to the sponsor to make sure that this doesn't (inadvertently) happen. Vets in particular are notorious for talking to the adult about the Junior's horse, even when the Junior is standing right there.

A confident Junior is comfortable talking to the vet on her own.

A tactful sponsor will re-direct the attention and conversation back to the Junior: "Amber is concerned that Tigger's pulse is higher than normal at the trot today. Amber, tell Dr. V what you normally see and how it is different today."

This gives the Junior an opportunity to share her observations, just as an adult rider would be expected to do. After a few interactions of this kind, the vets (and other adults) usually catch on and address their comments and concerns directly to the Junior, as they should.

What happens when the Juniors grow up? They have little Juniors of their own. And when those kids get old enough to ride endurance, their parents know exactly who to call and ask for sponsorship.

The Sponsor's Song

(to the tune of "Streets of Laredo")

As I was out walking my pony in ridecamp,
as I was out walking in ridecamp one day,
I spied a poor parent wrapped up in pink vet wrap,
with tears in his eyes, these words he did say,

"I see by your outfit that you sponsor Juniors,"
these words he did say as I boldly walked by.
"My pony is lame and I've broken my finger,
my kid needs a sponsor for tomorrow's ride."

"My kid, she rides well
and my kid, she is useful.
She'll watch for ribbons; she'll keep you on course.
She'll open up gates
and she'll close them behind you.
She'll boost you back up if you fall off your horse!"

I took the kid with me next morning at sunrise.
We rode through the day and we got to the end.
With one kid beside me I soon acquired others—
if you're sponsoring Juniors,
they'll tell all their friends!

So all of you riders with ponies beside you,
enjoy a good ride—take a Junior with you.
These kids can ride well and take care of their ponies.
They keep you awake—
and their parents will crew!

The kids, they are fun
and the kids, they are useful.
They'll trot-out your pony and keep you on course.
They'll sing you new songs, and they'll tell you new stories.
They'll boost you back up if you fall off your horse!

A good mentor can help you avoid the most common mistakes during your first years of competition. David LeBlanc and his horse Tsundances Laser are a "Decade Team," with much wisdom to share with new riders.

CHAPTER 15
DON'TS AND DOS FOR YOUR FIRST YEAR

The sport of endurance can seem so complicated when you're just starting out. Lots of people wonder what they should do and what they *shouldn't* do. This chapter contains the best advice to beginners I've come across, gathered from many experienced competitors.

DO win by completing; DON'T finish first

It takes more than a fast horse to finish first in a long-distance ride. Remember that in this sport, the horse that is first to cross the finish line is NOT necessarily the winner. In LD rides, the first horse to *pulse down* after crossing the finish line is considered the first finisher, even if *that* horse crossed the line 5th or 6th, behind other faster-moving equines. And even that horse isn't considered the winner until he has passed the final vet check. Pushing a horse too quickly over the finish line can result in non-completion.

In order to finish first, a horse must be extremely fit. Many top 10 LD ride finishers in my region are fit enough to complete a middle-of-the-pack 50-mile ride. However, there's a treacherously thin line between an extremely fit horse and one that is over-conditioned. Without a few years and many miles of experience in working with long-distance horses, it's difficult to judge which side of that line a particular equine falls on, and most newcomers to the sport err on the side of over-conditioning. Over-conditioning does much more harm than good. An over-conditioned horse is often thinner than the ideal, and his muscles and tendons are tired and more prone to injury. If your horse's weight drops below a score of 5 or 4 on the Henneke Body Condition scale (see chapter 7), if he seems lethargic or his coat develops a dull look, it is *imperative* that you back off on your conditioning. Either do fewer miles or slow down (or both) until his appetite returns and he is able to maintain weight and energy.

Remember also that it can take up to *2 years* to turn a pasture-potato into a fully legged-up and conditioned endurance horse. Rather than spend all that time training at home, bring your horse to camp so that he (and you) can learn the skills and routine of long-distance riding, and can compete together at a moderate pace as part of his conditioning. Leave first-place finishing to the experienced, canny riders who have trained their mounts over hundreds of miles and years of completions. In time, you may join their ranks.

It's not the prize that creates the smile—it's the knowledge that you've earned it!

Know this: most endurance riders could not tell you who won the last ride they attended. Most riders can't even remember who won the Tevis last year. But almost any rider can name more than one horse/rider team that has completed 5,000 miles or more together. If winning is your goal, set your sights on the long haul.

DO take care of your horse; DON'T break your horse

High-mileage rider Trilby Pedersen told me "Speed kills." She wasn't talking about cars (or drugs); she was talking about riding horses too fast.

Trilby knows how to ride slowly and still get her completions. She has accumulated many of her miles while finishing *dead last.* She explained to me that the way she figures it, she got a lot more ride for her entry fee because she used a lot more time to finish her miles. Her goal is always to finish with a healthy, happy horse, and she never worries about her placement. Trilby is almost always able to achieve her goal: as of this writing, she has more than 60,000 miles of completions on record.

As mentioned above, over-conditioned horses are much more prone to injury, including career-ending injuries. A good endurance horse can last a decade or more. Don't feel pressured to accrue all of his miles in the first season. Relax, enjoy the trail, and take care of your horse.

15.1: If your horse gets broken

This book emphasizes the need to proceed slowly and steadily through the training process to avoid injury to your noble steed. And yet, even when you do, occasionally things go wrong (see Chapter 13). It happens to most horses, in some way, at some point.

Do not *ever* feel self-conscious about calling the vet.

Whether you're at a ride or at home, your horse's best bet for recovery is immediate vet evaluation. Whether your horse has "found his rock" or he has a metabolic mishap, get the opinion of a vet as soon as possible. If possible, seek out an endurance vet, someone who has extensive experience with the injuries and recoveries specific to the sport. If the problem is lameness, your vet can help you design a recovery plan that lines up with the best practices for endurance, as well as suggest behavior and training changes that will minimize opportunity for re-injury. If the problem is metabolic, an endurance vet will ask about your feeding strategy and make suggestions that will help avoid recurrence.

DON'T break yourself; DO rest and have fun

Over-conditioning can happen to human athletes as well as equines. If your sleep is restless, if your stomach is upset, if you are distracted and over-stressed by your endurance goals, ease up. Give yourself permission to ride slower or less often. Take one or two rides off of your competition schedule and use that time to rest your muscles and heal your body.

Endurance is a sport, and it is supposed to be *fun.* If you are so stressed that you aren't enjoying yourself, re-evaluate your activities. Rethink your priorities and focus on spending a day of competition on scenic trails with your horse and your friends and a smile on your face.

Join regional groups of riders to meet more people and experience trails away from your usual haunts. Consider exploring other activities with your horse to break up the monotony of ride season. Move cattle, trot around some barrels, or just go for a ride with non-endurance friends and enjoy a day that doesn't involve thinking about speed goals, heart rates, and mileage.

DON'T stay home; DO volunteer

Volunteering doesn't have to cut into your training or competition schedule. If you can't bear to miss a ride, volunteer to assist ride management a day or two before an event—marking trails, setting up supplies, hauling water, and doing any of the thousands of jobs that need to be done before riders come to camp.

If you volunteer on ride day, management will be happy to hand you a stopwatch or a stethoscope, a pen and clipboard, or keys to the water truck. The skills you practice (and gain) will make you a better competitor, and your efforts will help keep rides running smoothly.

If you are injured during ride season, don't stay home! Ride management can always use more volunteers.

Organizations outside of the endurance community, like the Back Country Horsemen (one of the best known), also appreciate volunteers who aren't afraid to ride long trails to get to a work site. There may also be other local groups who would welcome you and your horse on a trail-building or trash-packing-out day. Get involved!

DON'T figure you know it all; DO be ready for a learning curve

Many riders come to endurance with years of knowledge and expertise in one or more unrelated equine disciplines. Becoming a beginner again is difficult for many people who are knowledgeable and successful in dressage, reining, jumping, or any other horse sport. Experienced horse people are accustomed to *knowing how to do things* with their horses, and they often balk (at least momentarily) at how the sport of endurance is conducted when the practices differ slightly—or significantly—from what they've experienced in other disciplines.

Keep your mind open and pay attention to how other riders successfully navigate the "endurance way." The rules of endurance do not require that newcomers change the way they train and interact or feed, transport, and house their horses. If your current regime works for you, then it's fine. However, if (or when) you encounter challenges (everyone does), be prepared to look around at the practice of experienced riders, to ask questions, and to change some stuff.

In more than a decade of training and competing, I have rarely had a routine day. With thousands of miles of experience, the game changes whenever you ride in a new location, take a new horse out, encounter a new weather pattern, or travel with a new riding partner. There is only one constant: the learning curve *never* stops.

DON'T neglect your brain; DO attend educational events

It may not sound appealing to drag yourself into a building to stand or sit still all day, but attending educational events such as Endurance 101 clinics or educational sessions at regional or national endurance conferences will move you further forward faster!

Endurance conventions offer educational opportunity, great vendors and the chance to spend time with other riders during the off-season.

Conferences often feature up-to-date and immediately useful information, including the latest research on endurance equine feeding strategies, first aid for horse and rider, trail building and maintenance, trailer safety, and rider fitness. Conferences are also a low-cost, fun way to get to know other competitors in the sport. Maybe you'll meet your endurance hero… or maybe you'll meet a new training buddy. If you skip the conferences, you'll never know what you missed: go (and learn) whenever you are able to.

Educational events do not need to be endurance-centric to be worth your while. If your local vet clinic hosts an equine first-aid workshop, be there! Seek out trail-building, saddle-fitting, or hoof-care classes. Attend horse expos. If you want to know about camping and wilderness survival, check the schedule of classes offered by local outdoor gear shops, community colleges, and parks departments.

While most of this does not apply directly to endurance riding, all of these skills can come in handy in the sport. Keep your mind open to new experiences and be ready to use new information to make your endurance experience better.

Mona Thacker has over 20 years of endurance experience, more than 10,000 AERC miles, and one of the best smiles in the sport.

CHAPTER 16
MANY KINDS OF WINNING

This chapter describes many of the best-known awards for endurance teams. And new awards are being created constantly. Most AERC awards reward members who ride long, ride carefully, and have fun. You should also check with regional organizations for additional awards they may offer. Then find one that suits your goals and prepare yourself to win!

"To Finish is to Win"

The most important kind of winning in endurance riding is summed up in the oft-repeated "To Finish is to Win." AERC rules state that every horse and rider team to *finish* the ride and complete the veterinary checkpoints must receive a prize. Sometimes the prizes are big and sometimes they are small, but all are recognition of a worthy accomplishment.

Tail end award

Not every ride awards a prize to the last-place finisher, but many do. I have collected an admirable heap of trinkets and toys by finishing dead-last over the years, including a rock painted like a turtle, a manure fork (designated the "rear-end" award), and a huge pile of flashlights. If you ride slowly enough, perhaps someday you will have an admirable heap of trinkets like mine.

Top 10

As mentioned in Chapter 15, I don't recommend that you try to place first in a ride during your first or second year of competition. Finish your rides, take care of your horse, have fun. After 2 or 3 years of solid completions, you may wish to pick up the pace and aim for finishing as one of the top 10. When you are ready to accelerate your training, I recommend that you read the e-book by longtime endurance competitor Dennis Summers, *4th Gear: Power Up Your Endurance Horse* (2012), which offers time-tested advice for competing safely at speed.

Bigger challenges: harder rides, longer distances, and multi-day events

One way to finish top 10 without dramatically altering your riding style is to enter longer-distance events. With the exception of high-profile rides like Tevis, Old Dominion, and the Big Horn 100, most 75- and 100-mile rides have fewer competitors, and thus, it's much easier to place in the top10! When you and your horse complete shorter distance events and look around at the finish line wondering what you will do to amuse yourselves for the remainder of the day, when your horse eats and drinks throughout the event, when he willingly returns to work at the end of a vet check, when he is "bright of eye and bushy of tail" the morning after an LD, consider entering a longer ride.

This rider will never forget her first year of competing.

Logically speaking, a 50-mile ride is twice as hard as a 25 miler, and in some ways this is true: ideally, you will travel the second half of your ride at the same speed as the first half, so you'll be out on the trail twice as long. However, it is interesting to note that while a 50 miler is more strenuous because you do the second half when you're a little more tired, some people find that doing 50s is not as difficult as they thought it would be, because the horse and rider who enter a 50 miler after doing some LD rides aren't really doing anything different—they're just doing a lot more of what they already know how to do.

Certainly, 50 milers (and 75 and 100 milers) are physically more taxing than LD rides, but often the biggest obstacles are mental. The rider, quite reasonably, may fear pushing the horse too hard or quickly, or the worry might be centered on the *rider's* ability to push through the longer distances. These are reasonable concerns; it is up to each individual rider to overcome them.

Riders looking for a longer-harder-bigger challenge may also consider multi-day rides. A multi-day ride might be as short as 2 days in a row or as long as 2 months, as in the case of "XP" rides held on the traditional Pony Express routes. Multi-day events are often laid back, low-pressure events, where horses and riders strive for a pace that will keep everyone happy and healthy over a long period of time. Some multi-day riders will bring two or more horses, and allow each horse a working day followed by a rest day. Others choose to ride the same horse for the duration of the event. Before entering a multi-day event, be sure that your horse has an adequate base of fitness, which usually takes a few years of distance riding to achieve.

Most multi-day rides offer extra awards to riders who compete every day of the event. These awards are not given to the swiftest horse of the day, but rather the steadiest finishers of the series.

100 milers

The ultimate endurance challenges are 100-mile events. The events of the Western States Trail Ride (Tevis), which traverses the Sierra Nevada mountains, the Big Horn 100 in Wyoming, and the Old Dominion in Virginia are commonly considered the most prestigious—and are generally recognized as the most physically taxing—events. Articles and even entire books could be (and have been) written about these rides. See the appendix for more information.

Best Condition (BC) award

Horses finishing in the top 10 of a ride are eligible for a Best Condition examination. This award is judged by the head vet based on a series of established criteria, and given to the horse considered to be fittest and freshest and in the soundest condition at the end of the ride, after being judged among and against a standard of well-conditioned, fit, and metabolically sound horses. The scoring is modified to include finishing time and weight factors in addition to the vet score. The vet may choose to not award a BC if he deems that no equine meets acceptable standards for it.

Best Condition horses are given points in the BC category of AERC, and a National Best Condition award is given at the end of each competitive year.

A proud rider and her happy horse model the halter and leadrope prize they won for Best Condition.

Breed and gender awards

Many breed associations want to encourage their members to participate in the sport of endurance and offer privately sponsored awards to horses and/or riders who qualify. If your noble steed is registered with any of the following breed associations, you may qualify for a year-end award: Akhal-Teke Association of North America, American Morgan Horse Association, American Saddlebred Registry, American Shagya Arabian Berband, American Paint Horse Association, American Quarter Horse Association, Appaloosa Horse Club, Arabian Horse Association, Foundation Appaloosa Horse Registry, Intermountain Wild Horse and Burro Advisors, Kentucky Mountain Saddle Horse Association, National Spotted Saddle Horse Association, North American Shagya-Arabian Society, Paso Fino Horse Association, Tennessee Walking Horses Breeders' and Exhibitors' Association, and the United States Trotting Association.

There are also national awards for competing mares ("The War Mare Award") and stallions ("Jim Jones Stallion Award"). Check and see if your regional ride association also has prizes in breed and gender categories.

Family and age-group awards

AERC offers a number of family and age-group awards, including awards for families competing together, husband and wife pairs, senior riders (over the age of 65), and Junior riders.

Check the AERC rule book or website for eligibility and rules. Other regional awards may exist as well; check with your regional organization for details.

Mileage awards, patches, and medallions

AERC offers rider mileage and equine mileage programs for members.

Rider Mileage Program. Upon completion of 250 miles, riders receive a Rider Mileage patch and a 250 mile chevron. Additional chevrons are awarded at 500, 750, and 1000 miles, and at each additional 1000 miles. Riders achieving these mileage plateaus are acknowledged in *Endurance News.*

Equine Mileage Program. Horses receive a medallion for each 1000 miles completed. Plateaus are acknowledged in *Endurance News.*

Limited Distance Program. Upon completion of 250 miles of LD rides, riders receive a Limited Distance Rider Mileage patch and a 250 mile chevron. Additional chevrons are awarded at 500, 750, and 1000 miles, and at each additional 1000 miles. Riders achieving these plateaus are acknowledged in *Endurance News*.

Limited Distance Equine Mileage Program. Upon completion of each 500 miles in LD sanctioned rides, the equine will be awarded a medallion. Plateaus are acknowledged in *Endurance News.*

Longevity awards

Prizes such as the "Pard'ners Award" and "Hall of Fame" are awarded to outstanding horses and riders who have shown significant performance and dedication to the sport through long years of successful competition.

Horses and horse/rider teams who have been performing for a long time may qualify for regional awards such as the "Tsyd Award" given to long-term horse and rider teams in the Pacific Northwest. Check with your regional associations to discover what prizes are available in this category.

"Decade Team"

The AERC "Decade Team" list was started in 2003 to recognize horse/rider teams who have competed together in distances of 50 miles or more for 10 years or longer. Interviews with "Decade Team" riders are permanently posted on the AERC website and contain much wisdom about training and the sport.

"Perfect Ten"

The exclusive "Perfect Ten" award was created in 1997 and sponsored by Hall of Fame member Joe Long. This award recognizes horses that have completed 10 years of competition (or more), 10,000 miles (or more), 10 first-place finishes, and 10 Best Condition awards. As of this writing, only seven horses have achieved "Perfect Ten" status.

Becoming an endurance rider may seem like one of the most daunting tasks you have ever set yourself, but it is entirely achievable. No matter how many or how few miles you and your equine partner complete over the years, you're accomplishing something great. There's no feeling as satisfying as guiding a fit horse through an arduous event, and no smile like the smile of a successful endurance rider at the finish line.

See you on the trail!

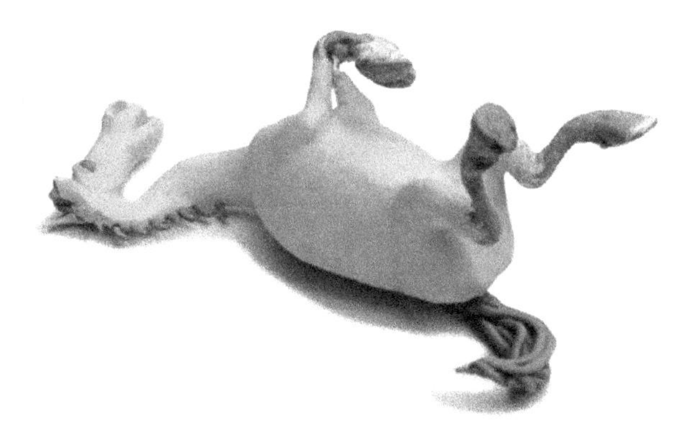

GLOSSARY

ADR – "Ain't doing right." A catchall term used by veterinarians for a health condition that shows no overt symptoms, but is distinctly sub-normal.

AHF – "Ain't having fun." An unofficial but perfectly legitimate reason to quit doing something that is not enjoyable.

Biothane – a synthetic polyvinyl-coated polyester webbing. Also beta biothane, a similar material with a thicker, more leather-like appearance and texture.

BPM – "beats per minute," used in measuring heart rates.

Bute - Phenylbutazone, often referred to as bute, is a non-steroidal anti-inflammatory drug (NSAID) for the short-term treatment of pain and fever in animals.

Cages (stirrup) – enclosures attached to a stirrup to prevent a rider's foot from sliding all the way through a stirrup.

Cavalletti – poles or branches on the ground used for trot-over practice.

Cardiac Recovery Index – a comparative measurement of the horse's heart rate before and 60 seconds after a 250-foot trot-out. Also called a "CRI" or a "Ridgeway Trot."

Confirmation -- establishing [something] as true. Ratification; verification.

Conformation – the structure or form of a thing.

Crew bag (or crew box) – the supplies needed for a vet check, stored in a bag or box and hopefully weighing 30 pounds or less.

CRI - a comparative measurement of the horse's heart rate before and 60 seconds after a 250-foot trot-out. Also called a "Cardiac Recovery Index" or "Ridgeway Trot."

DIMR – "Distance-Induced Mental Retardation." The combination of dehydration, fatigue and highway hypnosis which causes long-distance riders to become extremely stupid.

Down – when a horse's heart rate reaches the mandatory criteria (usually 60 or 64 bpm), he is considered "down." This information is relayed to the ride timer, who will provide a "down-time" to be recorded on the rider card.

Endurance ride – a long-distance ride of fifty miles or longer.

Emancipation - a rider 14 years or older who has completed 500 AERC miles or more (in any distance) may "emancipate" in order to ride without a sponsor. The emancipation process requires that the junior and his/her parent write a letter to the AERC office well in advance of an event, consenting to and requesting the unsponsored status. Emancipated juniors ride in the senior division. A ride manager does not have to honor the emancipation.

Full distance – an endurance ride, fifty miles or longer.

Gaited horse – a horse who displays one or more "easy gaits." An easy gait is a four-beat gait executed at the speed of a trot. Examples of gaited horse breeds include but are not limited to Icelandic Horses, Missouri Fox Trotters, Paso Finos, and Tennessee Walking Horses. Individuals in other breeds not known for gaitedness may exhibit easy gait also.

Heart rate monitor – also called HRM, an electronic device used to measure and monitor a subject's heart rate. Equine heart rate monitors usually include electrode patches which secure beneath the saddle and send data to a transmitter, which then sends data to a wristwatch or hand-held monitor that can be conveniently read while on the move or at a vet-check.

Henneke Body Condition Scoring - The system developed by Dr. Don Henneke assigns a numerical value to fat deposition as it occurs in various places on the horse's body. The system works by assessing fat both visually and by palpation (examination by touch), in each of six areas.

Herd-bound horse – a herd-bound horse does not like to be out of sight, or even very distant from, familiar horses.

Hoof boots – protective coverings for horse hooves, used in addition to, or in place of, traditional steel shoes. Common brands of hoof boots include EasyBoot, Old Mac, and Renegade boots.

Junior rider – A rider under the age of 16. Special rules apply to juniors, and special awards are often available.

LD – "Limited Distance," a long-distance ride of 25 miles or longer, but less than 50 miles. Limited Distance events are usually 25 to 35 miles long.

Leg up – to condition a horse in distance work so that he is fit to carry a rider in endurance competition.

Limited Distance – a long-distance ride of 25 miles or longer, but less than 50 miles. Limited Distance events are usually 25 to 35 miles long. Also called an "LD ride."

Novice ride – a shortened version of an endurance event, usually 8-15 miles. The novice distance is often used as an introductory ride for horse or rider (or both). Although events at this distance do not award points to the team when completed, a completion prize is usually given. Also called a "fun ride."

Out-check – a vet check that occurs away from the main ridecamp. Also called an "out-vet" or "out-vet-check."

P&R – pulse and respiration. This label also applies to the volunteer who measures these, called a "P&R person" or a "P/R" or a "pulser."

Pulser – the person (usually a trained volunteer, not a veterinarian) who uses a stethoscope to measure a horse's pulse.

Quad – a four-wheeled all-terrain vehicle. Also called a "quadrunner" or "ATV."

Rating – the ability to control a horse's speed at any gait. A horse who "rates well" can be asked to execute a particular gait at a specific speed without continual reminders to maintain that gait and that speed.

Ride manager – the person (or team) in charge of every aspect of running a specific ride. This person is the ultimate authority, and also a minor deity, without whom the sport could not happen. Also called an "RM."

Ridecamp – the trailhead where endurance riders gather for an event. Also, a high-traffic international online discussion group dedicated to endurance and long-distance riding - www.endurance.net/ridecamp

Ridgeway Trot – also called the "Cardiac Recovery Index" or "CRI," a comparative measurement of the horse's heart rate before and 60 seconds after a 250-foot trot-out.

RM – "Ride Manager."

RO-L – "Rider Option – Lame." The pull-code for a horse removed from competition for lameness by the rider *after he has passed the veterinary exam.*

RO-M – "Rider Option – Metabolic." The pull-code for a horse removed from competition for metabolic reasons by the rider *after he has passed the veterinary exam.*

RO – "Rider Option." The pull code for a horse removed from competition because the *rider* is too sick, injured, or AHF to continue the event.

Sponsor – a responsible adult over the age of 21 who rides with a junior in a distance event.

Tailing – with the horse in front and the rider behind on the ground, the horse pulls the rider (who holds onto the horse's tail as well as to a long rein or "tailing rope" attached to the halter), usually up or down a steep hill.

Tevis – the popular name for the 100-mile Western States Trail Ride. Tevis is held during the full-moon weekend of July or August each year, along one of the toughest courses in the United States.

Thumps – "Synchronous Diaphragmatic Flutter," which is a warning sign of serious fluid and electrolyte imbalance. When a horse is thumping, the electrical signal for the heart to contract is also conducted through the phrenic nerve and the diaphragm contracts with each heartbeat. When looking at the horse, it is possible to see the thumps or contraction of the diaphragm with each heartbeat.

Towel – a towel is most massively useful thing an endurance rider can have. You can wrap it around you for warmth as you wait for the start time; you can lie on it on the brilliant marble-sanded beaches of the vet checks of Western Oregon, you can sleep under it beneath the stars of the Biltmore. You can wave your towel in emergencies as a distress signal, and of course, dry yourself off with it if it still seems to be clean enough.

Vet check – a pitstop for the horse, where equines are evaluated by a veterinarian according to AERC criteria. Vet checks may take place in the main ridecamp, or at designated locations along the trail.

FOOTNOTED RESOURCES

All links current at time of publication.

Chapter One

AERC Rules and Regulations. Auburn, CA. 2012.

Suhr, Julie. *Ten Feet Tall, Still.* Scott Valley, CA : Marinera Pub., 2002.

Chapter Two

AERC Rules and Regulations. Auburn, CA. 2012.

"Helmet Safety." Equestrian Medical Safety Association. EMSA. October 5, 2012. Web. www.emsaonline.net/helmet_safety.html

Endurance.Net. Ridecamp discussion group. Web. www.endurance.net/ridecamp (an account is required)

Eng, Ronald C. *Mountaineering: the Freedom of the Hills* (8th edition). Seattle : Mountaineers Books, 2010.

Tanner, Dave (Director). Every Time, Every Ride (film). Puyallup, WA : Washington State University Cooperative Extension and Washington State 4-H Foundation, 1995.

Chapter Three

"ACTHA Obstacles." ACTHA: American Competitive Trail Horse Association. American Competitive Trail Horse Association. October 5, 2012. Web. https://www.actha.us/obstacles

Chapter Seven

"Body Conditioning Scoring for Your Horse." 2002. University of Maine Cooperative Extension Publications, January 25, 2012. Web. umaine.edu/publications/1010e/

Geor, Ray RSc, PhD, Dipl. ACVIM. "Spring Tuning (Athletic Conditioning)." February 01, 2001. theHorse.com, January 24, 2012. Web. www.thehorse.com/ViewArticle.aspx?ID=226

Geor, Ray RSc, PhD, Dipl. ACVIM. "Getting Your Horse in Shape." February 01, 2002. theHorse.com, January 24, 2012. Web. **www.thehorse.com/ViewArticle.aspx?ID=3263**

Steelman, Samantha PhD. "10 Principles of Exercise Physiology." June 01, 2008. theHorse.com, January 24, 2012. Web. www.thehorse.com/ViewArticle.aspx?ID=12094

West, Christy M. "AAEP Convention: Milne Lecture — Bucked Shins." February 27, 2003. theHorse.com, January 24, 2012. Web. www.thehorse.com/ViewArticle.aspx?ID=4066&src=topic

Chapter Eight

Haydt, Eric. "Understanding Beet Pulp as an Equine Feed." September 07, 2009. theHorse.com, July 07, 2012. Web. www.thehorse.com/ViewArticle.aspx?ID=14812

Garlinghouse, Susan DVM. "Beet Pulp Safety Warning (aka the famous squirrel story)." 1997. July 07, 2012.Web. www.endurance-101.com/garlinghouse/Beet_Pulp_Safety_Warning.pdf

Wood, Craig H. "Condition Scoring for Your Horse." April, 1995. July 07, 2012. Web. www.uky.edu/Ag/AnimalSciences/pubs/asc145.pdf

Chapter Nine

Stuart, Ann DVM. "Thoughts on electrolytes and equine athletes." March, 2008. Aerc.org, February 03, 2012.Web. www.aerc.org/ENMarch-08Vet.asp

"Unwritten Rules." Ride Stories. March 24, 2000. Endurance.Net. October 5, 2012. Web.
stories.endurance.net/2000/03/unwritten-rules.html

Chapter Eleven

Summers, Dennis. *Fourth Gear: Power Up Your Endurance Horse.* Animal House, 2012.

Garlinghouse, Susan DVM. "Beating the Metabolic Pull — Part 1: Hydration." Endurance News, June 2000.
www.endurance-101.com/garlinghouse/Beating_the_Metabolic_Pull_Part-I.pdf

Chapter Twelve

Garlinghouse, Susan DVM. "Alfalfa for Distance Horses."1998. July 07, 2012. Web.
www.endurance-101.com/garlinghouse/Alfalfa_for_Distance_Horses.pdf

Chapter Thirteen

AERC Rules and Regulations, rule 13 (drug policy). Auburn, CA. 2012

APPENDIX A: USEFUL RESOURCES

NATIONAL AND REGIONAL DISTANCE RIDING ORGANIZATIONS

This non-comprehensive list is intended to give readers a starting place to find endurance rides and riders in their region. To find the more complete list maintained by the AERC, search online for the terms: "AERC organizations." Many groups also maintain an unofficial presence on Facebook.

American Endurance Rides Conference

www.aerc.org -- The umbrella organization of endurance riding in the United States and Canada.

AERC Central Region

www.aerccentralregion.org --The Central Region hosts its own website and celebrates the accomplishments of AERC riders from Arkansas, Kansas, Louisiana, Missouri, Oklahoma and Texas.

Mountain Region Endurance Riders

www.mrer.org -- MRER is the regional endurance riding organization for the Mountain Region. Members participate in an awards program and receive a bi-monthly newsletter.

Ozark Country Endurance Riders (Arkansas, Kansas, Missouri, Oklahoma: Central Region)

ocer.us -- OCER is a regional club which sponsors limited distance and endurance rides in the states of Arkansas, Kansas, Missouri, and Oklahoma.

South Eastern Distance Riding Association (Florida: Southeast Region)

www.distanceriding.org - SEDRA sanctions distance events and maintains records for the benefit of its members, recognizing annual high point athletes and lifetime mileage accrual awards for riders and horses. SEDRA actively provides a wide variety of clinics to improve the horse/rider team and dedicates funds and volunteer hours to trails, trail cleanup and preservation.

Southeast Endurance Riders Association (Southeast Region)

www.seraonline.org -SERA is a non-profit organization designed to promote endurance riding, encourage better care of endurance horses through rider education and assist ride managers in producing quality competitions.

Southwest Distance Riders Association (Southwest Region)

sports.groups.yahoo.com/group/swdra --SWDRA shares ideas, ride calendars, stories, etc. The group also awards accomplishments on an annual basis.

Upper Midwest Endurance & Competitive Riders Association (Midwest Region)

www.umecra.com -- UMECRA was formed with the goal of promoting the sport of endurance and competitive riding and good horsemanship, and standardized a set of rules for the rides to reduce variation in the way rides were managed, to coordinate ride dates, to tally points, and to present year-end awards at an annual banquet.

CANADA

Distance Riders of Manitoba Association (Midwest Region)

www.kucera.mb.ca/drma -- The DRMA, which is associated with the Manitoba Horse Council, promotes endurance riding in the province of Manitoba and brings together equestrians interested in the sport. Benefits include a mileage program, annual awards, and a newsletter.

Endurance Riders of Alberta (Mountain Region)

www.enduranceridersofalberta.com -- Endurance Riders of Alberta (ERA) is a sanctioning, record-keeping, and awards body for riders and horses competing in endurance events in Alberta.

Endurance Riders of British Columbia (Northwest Region)

www.erabc.com -- Each year ERABC awards mileage awards, high point horse and rider and high point B.C. awards as well as awards for consistency at the association's general meeting. There is a bi-annual ERABC newsletter.

Equine Canada

www.equinecanada.ca -- EC represents all equestrian disciplines and equine activity in Canada. In addition to a system of over 600 competitions across Canada, the disciplines offer athlete development and high performance programs to provide support to those progressing through the competitive system.

Ontario Competitive Trail Riding Association (Northeast Region)

www.octra.on.ca -- OCTRA sanctions endurance rides, competitive trail rides and ride & ties in Ontario.

CONNECT WITH ENDURANCE RIDERS ONLINE

Bloggers:

This is another non-comprehensive list. Explore the sidebars of these blogs to find links to other blogs.

BootsandSaddles4Mel: www.bootsandsaddles4mel.com/

Merri Melde: theequestrianvagabond.blogspot.com/

Karen Chaton: enduranceridestuff.com/blog/

Aarene Storms: haikufarm.blogspot.com

Heather Reynolds: www.reynoldsracing.us/heathers_blog

Monica Bretherton: blog.seattlepi.com/horsebytes/

In the Night Farm: inthenightfarm.wordpress.com/

MONK: feiredhorse.blogspot.com/

It Seemed Like a Good Idea at the Time: fundersgoodidea.blogspot.com/

Discussion groups:

Ridecamp: The grandparent of all endurance discussion groups, an international discussion of long-distance riding www.endurance.net/Ridecamp/

New 100's: A group for new (and aspiring) 100-mile riders and their mentors -- sports.groups.yahoo.com/group/new100milers/

Gaited: A group for riders of gaited horses in endurance -- pets.dir.groups.yahoo.com/group/GaitedEnduranceRiders/

Barefoot Endurance Horses: A discussion group for riders interested in keeping horses shoeless -- sports.dir.groups.yahoo.com/group/BarefootEnduranceHorses/

Tack and Equipment Vendors

Online tack companies come and go. To locate a list of current and complete list of vendors selling everything from horses to horse property, saddles, boots, breeches, and trucks, please visit www.endurance.net/market/index.html

Action Rider Tack: www.actionridertack.com/

American Trail Gear: www.americantrailgear.com/

Distance Depot: www.thedistancedepot.com/

EasyCare: www.easycareinc.com/

Griffin's Tack: www.griffinstack.com

Hought Endurance Tack: www.hought.com/endthg.html

Long Rider's Gear: www.longridersgear.com/

Moss Rock Endurance: www.mossrockendurance.com/

Running Bear: www.runningbear.com/

TTeam for Endurance: www.tteamforendurance.com/Pages/default.aspx

Books

Independent booksellers and public libraries can often track down hard-to-find or out-of-print titles.

Hollander, Lew and Ingram, Patricia. **Successful Endurance Riding. Penguin Group, 1981.** *Out of print.* Maximize the performance of your horse and yourself by proper conditioning, preparation, and race strategies. Revised edition: **Endurance Riding : from beginning to winning,** *also out of print.*

Hyland, Ann. **Riding Long Distance.** Robert Hale, Ltd., 1992. A guide for those wishing to combine the pleasure of a long ride with the excitement of competition.

Langer, Marnye. **The Tevis Cup: To Finish Is To Win.** Globe Pequot Press, 2005. *Out of print.* This book is a history of the Tevis trail, the riders and the horses.

Loving, Nancy S. **Go the Distance: The Complete Resource for Endurance Horses.** Trafalgar Square Books, 2006. A definitive guide to long distance riding, written by a leading equine veterinarian and endurance ride official.

Paulo, Karen. **America's Long Distance Challenge.** Penguin Group, 1990. *Out of print.* Many beautiful photos make for a wonderful pictoral history of Endurance Riding with many pictures from the Tevis and the Race of Champions.

Savitt, Sam. **One Horse, One Hundred Miles, One Day.** Dodd, Mead & Co, 1981. *Out of print.*
The story of the Tevis Cup, a one hundred mile horse race held in California over the course of one day.

Snyder-Smith, Donna. **The Complete Guide to Endurance Riding and Competition.** Howell Book House, 1998. This thorough guide provides information to keep horse and rider on the right path.

Suhr, Julie. **Ten Feet Tall, Still.** Marinera Press, 2002. One woman's journey from childhood to old age in a life of joy and passion with horses.

Summers, Dennis. **4th Gear: Power Up Your Endurance Horse.** Animal House, 2012, E-book.

INDEX

I

J

L

M

O

P

R

S

T

V

W

About the Author

Author Aarene Storms returned to horses as an adult after wasting her teen years becoming educated and employed. In 1999 she rode her first long-distance event on an short and opinionated Standardbred mare called Story. She has been active in the endurance community ever since.

An advocate for junior riders, equestrian trails, and novice endurance horse-and-rider teams, Aarene has written numerous articles for *Endurance News* and other equestrian publications. Her adventures in the saddle and on the ground are documented with tongue firmly-in-cheek at the Haiku Farm blog.

Aarene now rides in the Pacific Northwest region on a tall and opinionated Standardbred mare called Fiddle.

She is available for Endurance 101 mini-clinics and speaking engagements. Please contact her at bookings@endurance-101.com.

Photographer Monica Bretherton has been hoarding endurance pictures for quite some time while riding other people's horses. Most recently, she has been seen at endurance rides with Magdan (Danny), whom she borrows from Cascade Gold Akhal-Tekes. Their adventures are sometimes chronicled in her own blog, hosted at the Seattle PI, Horsebytes. You can reach her via Triangle Ranch Communications.

She also has taken the only known images of Purpaloosas and is the acknowledged worldwide expert on their misbehavior.

Share This Book

There's no better way to enjoy endurance riding than with a friend.

If you want to send a gift copy of either the print edition,

the e-book or the e-book on CD,

you may order online at www.endurance-101.com

CPSIA information can be obtained
at www.ICGtesting.com
Printed in the USA
BVHW062307191221
624488BV00015B/403